Praise

Take Good Care of the Garden and the Dogs

"Here is the real thing—good old-fashioned American values coming from small-town Alaska. In a cozy, chatty voice, Heather Lende tells stories of life in Haines, Alaska . . . Accepting life and rejoicing in the world are her preferred modes of thinking and feeling."   —*The Boston Globe*

"[Lende's book] is about her community and her family, the supporters who helped her get back on her feet with love, compassion, faith and humor . . . Her writing style is crisp and clear."   —*The Seattle Times*

"Heather Lende continues to explore small-town life in the last frontier, with profound reflections on motherhood, mercy, and the art of mending. *Take Good Care of the Garden and the Dogs* will touch your heart and soul and give you much to think about long after you've turned the last page."
    —Jo-Ann Mapson, author of *The Owl & Moon Café*

"*Take Good Care of the Garden and the Dogs* celebrates the resilience of ordinary people, gathered together to help one another with the business of living and dying. Reading this memoir is like listening to an old friend . . . The effect is pleasantly intimate, as if we were sitting next to her on the Juneau ferry."   —*BookPage*

"A multilevel look at serendipity, coincidence, irony and the power of friendship and faith."

—*Rocky Mount (NC) Telegram*

"Fifteen well turned essays about living in the shadow of death in a world both harsh and beautiful . . . An uplifting, even cheerful book. Lende has a knack for subtly illuminating the remarkable in the commonplace, the transcendence in tragedy . . . Her voice, which alternates between folksy and formal, playful and prayerful, entertaining and elegiac, is reminiscent of Garrison Keillor, Krista Tippett, Tom Bodett, Kathleen Norris and Anne Lamott. But Lende has a freshness that keeps her from being too derivative, and Alaska's geography, history and culture strongly flavor her work."

—*Minneapolis Star Tribune*

"[Lende] conveys in her newest book, *Take Good Care of the Garden and the Dogs,* the importance of spirituality and community in life's lessons."   —*Alaska* magazine

"Lende writes emotionally but never sentimentally, giving us the best Alaska memoir of late, maybe the best ever."

—*Booklist,* starred review

"The book is full of vivid characters (a librarian who collects overdue books in person) and strange, sad deaths. Lende is not one for looking back. She has a simple, chatty style most readers will find oddly comforting. Life does, in fact, go on." —*Los Angeles Times*

"[Lende] proves a skilled observer of nature in the wild and nature in human form . . . Her cozy whimsy is refreshing . . . Amiable in Alaska and slightly left of center, projecting the warmth of a well-made campfire." —*Kirkus Reviews*

"This book is a wonder. It opens a door to Alaskan living, a world that, for most, will be both surprising and beautiful. As a person of Alaska and a person of faith, it is one of the best books of theology and spirituality that I have read in a long time. But the non-religious or the non-Alaskan shouldn't be hesitant. They will also be glad to walk through this door to a world that is certainly and recognizably theirs, but will seem to hold much more— maybe things new or maybe things forgotten."
—The Rt. Rev. Mark MacDonald, formerly
the Bishop of Alaska, now the National
Indigenous Anglican Bishop of Canada

Take Good Care of
the Garden and the Dogs

ALSO BY HEATHER LENDE

If You Lived Here, I'd Know Your Name:
News from Small-Town Alaska

Take Good Care of
the Garden and the Dogs

*A True Story of Bad Breaks
and Small Miracles*

HEATHER LENDE

ALGONQUIN BOOKS OF CHAPEL HILL 2011

Published by
ALGONQUIN BOOKS OF CHAPEL HILL
Post Office Box 2225
Chapel Hill, North Carolina 27515-2225

a division of
WORKMAN PUBLISHING
225 Varick Street
New York, New York 10014

First paperback edition, Algonquin Books of Chapel Hill, April 2011.
Originally published by Algonquin Books of Chapel Hill in 2010.
Printed in the United States of America.
Published simultaneously in Canada
by Thomas Allen & Son Limited.

The Library of Congress has cataloged
the hardcover edition of this book as follows:
Lende, Heather, [date]
Take good care of the garden and the dogs : family, friendships, and
faith in small-town Alaska / by Heather Lende.— 1st ed.
p. cm.
ISBN 978-1-56512-568-1 (HC)
1. Lende, Heather, [date]   2. Lende, Heather, [date]—Family.
3. Lende, Heather, [date]—Friends and associates.   4. Lende,
Heather, [date]—Religion.   5. Faith.   6. Haines (Alaska)—
Biography.   7. Haines (Alaska)—Social life and customs.
8. City and town life—Alaska—Haines.   9. Outdoor
life—Alaska—Haines.   10. Frontier and pioneer life—
Alaska—Haines.   I. Title.
F914.H34L47 2010
979.8'2051092—dc22
[B]   2010002100

ISBN 978-1-61620-051-0 (PB)

10 9 8 7 6 5 4 3 2 1
First Paperback Edition

For my father, Robert Vuillet,
and in memory of my mother,
Sarah Jane Smith Vuillet,
August 26, 1934–April 20, 2006

CONTENTS

ACKNOWLEDGMENTS

Haines, Alaska, and the Chilkat Valley are known for exceptional scenery and wildlife, but the people are even more extraordinary. I have lived here for all of my adult life and until fairly recently, as you will soon read, have never been on the receiving end of the community's care and generosity. Without all the help and support our family and I were given, this book would not have been written. I am more grateful than words can convey. I'm afraid to list everyone who helped me back on my feet physically and emotionally because I'll surely miss someone. Please consider this story my gift to you.

I do want to name the people who contributed to the work of writing and publishing this book: Amy Gash, my wise, faithful, and very patient editor, and everyone else at Algonquin; my editors past and present at the *Anchorage Daily News*, Kathleen McCoy, Julie Wright, Mark Dent, and Mike Dunham; Tom Morphet, editor of the *Chilkat Valley News*; Valerie Miner, my mentor from the University of Alaska, Anchorage, creative writing program; Nancy Nash, Liz Heywood, and Sarah "Tigger" Posey, who read each page and carefully corrected grammar and spelling mistakes I made; gentle readers Ellen Borders, Beth MacCready, Jo-Ann Mapson, and Melina Shields; Matt Davis for the great photo; my family near and far, especially Chip; and, finally, the Reverend Jan Hotze of St. Michael and All Angels Episcopal Mission. Thank you all for showing me, as Jan says, "All is Grace."

Take Good Care of
the Garden and the Dogs

CHAPTER 1

Grant Us Wisdom, Grant Us Courage

Dear God, have mercy on me.
The sea is so wide and my boat is so small.
—Fisherman's Prayer

The first day of spring was not March 20, and it wasn't one day but a handful of early April days so bright that the residents of this little seaside Alaskan town crawled blinking out of our snow caves and welcomed it like sleepy bears. Spring fever hit so hard that everyone was smiling and doing their best to push winter out the door. Blankets and pillows were aired, decks were shoveled, and icy walks were chipped off. Anglers post-holed through the snowy riverbanks to cast for the first fat Dolly Vardens. The Public Works Department foreman even took a snow-blowing plow truck to the high school track and carved out a four-hundred-meter oval in the shoulder-high snow so the team could practice.

On Sunday afternoon, I walked in the dripping sunshine to the annual Blessing of the Fleet. Actually, it was only the third or fourth blessing of the Haines harbor fishing boats that I can recall in my twenty-five years in Haines, but it may become yearly if this one works out. It's not that we don't all support the idea of an annual blessing, but community events require organizing and advertising and choir practicing and program printing and cookie baking for the inevitable reception following. This one also needs a nice day and well-spoken ministers. What I mean to say is, traditions don't just happen. People make them happen and, for all kinds of good reasons, some years they do and some years they don't.

As I walked to town, I realized that spring truly was here because no one asked if I wanted a ride. Even casual drivers-by could see it was a fine day for a walk. One pickup truck passed me, slowed down, and then parked at the bottom of Cemetery Hill, where my neighbors hopped out and took a stroll down Mud Bay Road, smiling at the views of the Chilkat Inlet, Pyramid Island, and the snowy mountains that look the way the Alps would, if Switzerland had a beach.

I was more than a little relieved that this April was already so much better than the last two. I'd been starting to think that April might really be a cursed month. April 2005 should have been terrific. My first book was just about to be released and my oldest daughter, Eliza, was just about to graduate from Bowdoin College in Maine. We were planning the book tour around her graduation. That way, I could start on the East Coast and make my way back home. In preparation, I had bought a suitcase with wheels and a pair of nice shoes that I could walk in. On Thursday, April 7, I volunteered to host the local morning radio program—two hours of playing music, reading the announcements and weather, and keeping everyone in Haines, Skagway, and the nearby Tlingit village of Klukwan company.

After the show, since it was such a nice warm morning (about forty-five degrees by eleven o'clock), I took my bike out for the second ride of the season. I was thinking about what I'd say when Oprah interviewed me about my book (not likely, but, just in case, I wanted to be ready) when I saw a truck stopped at the stop sign on an otherwise quiet cross street overlooking the harbor. The driver, Kevin from the grocery store, glanced both ways, and seeing no cars (or, apparently, cyclists), pulled out and ran me over. I was medevaced to Seattle's Harborview Trauma Center and put back together. I spent three weeks in a nursing home there and another ten weeks confined to a bed or a wheelchair in my living room. By Halloween, I was able to walk without crutches but was still frequenting physical therapy, acupuncture, and massage therapy sessions once a week. These would continue until January. (I'll tell you all about it later.)

Just as I was feeling almost like myself again, my mother's chronic lymphocytic leukemia went bad, really bad. I spent the rest of that winter and spring going back and forth between Alaska and my parents' home in New

York. I was on my way there on April 7, 2006. She died on April 20.

This April had no dark cloud over it, so far, and I have never seen a piano or a safe being hauled into an upper-story window with a block and tackle in Haines (or anywhere except in those Wile E. Coyote cartoons), so I wasn't anxiously checking for one to fall on my head. Still, as I walked down the quiet road, I gave passing vehicles plenty of room and tried not to jump when a truck with a loud muffler roared up behind me. I did think that praying for other people to be spared accidents or death (for a season, anyway) at the Blessing of the Fleet was a positive way to honor my tender feelings. I am not the same person I was three Aprils ago. I'm still an awkward hugger and may always be, but at least now I *want* to hug people.

The ceremony began so perfectly that I knew I'd been right to come. It was well organized, simple, dignified, and featured plain prayers that didn't ask for more than what was possible, beginning with "Dear God, have mercy on me. The sea is so wide and my boat is so small." It appeared that there would not be, as my mother used to say, any "wailing or gnashing of teeth" over the departed today. The Salvation Army captain was in his festive red and black dress uniform with the long overcoat and ribbon-trimmed cap, the Catholic priest wore his black shirt and pants and white collar under a thick fleece jacket, and the Presbyterian pastor had on a warm coat, jeans, and brown rubber fishing boots. In the harbor parking lot, the wind off Lynn Canal was still cold, but the sun was warm enough that water was running everywhere, off nearby roofs and down drainage ditches.

The first hymn was "Praise to the Lord, the almighty, the king of creation," and we all sang from the words printed in our leaflets. It started me thinking about the beginnings of life, of spring and birth. It is often said that there are no atheists in foxholes. It seems to me that shelled bunkers would be full of skeptics. In the middle of a war it must be harder, not easier, to believe in a good God. If it were up to me, I'd change that line to there are no atheists in delivery rooms or adoption agencies, but maybe that's because I have given birth to four children and have adopted one. Maybe. I do know for certain that to witness spring hit Haines and the Chilkat Valley is as close as I'll come to being present at the birth of the world. The words we often use to describe our Alaskan landscape are even biblical: majestic mountains, shining seas, rivers cleft from rocks. We actually have leviathans—humpback and killer whales—in our deep, and we know what it means to soar on eagle wings. All we have to do is look out the window.

THE MEN OF NOTE, an a cappella chorus of a dozen or so guys directed by Bob Plucker—retired music professor from the Midwest—that includes a fisherman, a physicist from Los Alamos, the school maintenance man, a minister, a couple of high school boys, and a heavy equipment operator, sang so well that everyone clapped when they finished, even though it was a kind of open-air church service.

But then, as often happens when all is right with the weather and with the community and with my heart, everything veered dangerously off course. The bell at the Presbyterian church across the street began tolling, once for each death the previous year, and every name was read out loud as their loved ones each dropped a flower in a straw laundry basket that would be floated off the dock after the service.

I had thought that we were praying for the future, that we were launching into a new season on the water, that we were looking forward with hope, not aft in sadness. I like the idea of blessing commercial fishing boats, kayaks, sailboats, and even ferries. I see no harm at all in saying prayers, sprinkling holy water, or wafting incense out over all the boats in town. What a good deed to do. Of course, I could see how we might want to remember those who had died at sea since the last blessing. There could be a moment of silence before the festivities, but the thing is, no one had died at sea last year. I know this for certain because I write the obituaries in this town, and the editor at the *Chilkat Valley News,* my friend Tom Morphet, insists on my reporting detailed causes of death. No one in Haines dies of "natural causes." As Tom says, a heart attack is natural; so is a brain tumor and so is drowning, but they are very different ways to die. Which brings me back to my point. No one had died in water anywhere near Haines the previous year. I had thought that this was a very good sign. It meant the hymns and prayers from the previous blessing had worked. Maybe that's what explained the big turnout.

All had gone well for twelve whole months. True, Guy Hoffman did die on Chilkoot Lake, but he didn't even get wet. Losing Guy was a shock. He wasn't old and he wasn't sick and he was mostly happy. It was Guy who said that if you want nice weather, then make your own high-pressure system, and he did. Guy was skiing across the lake on a beautiful, sunny late-winter day with two of his closest friends when his big heart stopped and he lay down in the snow and died. But his name was still called at the Blessing of the Fleet, because every single person who had died in Haines or nearby Klukwan—in bed, in cars, in the hospital, watching *Everybody Loves Raymond,* as Gene Philpott had—was announced. So were the names of many more people who hadn't died here but were dead nonetheless. They had been related to or were friends of people who live here. They even added the dead from the first few months of this year, just to be sure no one was forgotten and maybe in case we don't have a formal Blessing of the Fleet next year.

Well, there were more than you'd think.

But that was not all. When the representatives of the Haines Ministerial Association finished with the recently

dead, they went back to the theme of the day and began calling the names of everyone who had ever drowned
in our sea, rivers, lakes, or swimming holes. "The Sul-
livan family," the pastor said, and then read the names
of the seven Sullivans, all of whom (and their dog) had
died before I moved to Haines when their skiff capsized
on the way home from a beach picnic in an unexpected
afternoon squall. By now my soul's own little sloop was
sideslipping toward the rocks.

T. S. Eliot wrote that April is the cruelest month. You
know, with all due respect, it is not the best month for
me, either. I do not want to remember my accident or my
mother's death. I want to remember my recovery and the
way my mother was before she was so sick.

So I stood and half-listened. The voices reading the
names sounded as if they were underwater. I watched
an eagle circling high above the boats in the harbor. I
watched that bird and let my heart go with it, gracefully
looping higher and higher. I remembered that sharing my
story about my own terribly bad times had helped me. I
remembered that it had made them bearable and allowed
me to appreciate the good parts of my story even more. I
also realized that most of us have been hit by a proverbial
truck at least once and that, as broadsides go, mine may
have been one of the easier to recover from because it was
so literal and so public, compared to breast cancer or a
messy divorce.

I write a weekly Thursday column for the *Anchorage Daily News,* in the Family & Life section. I write about anything I want to: Haines, my family, community goings-on. I try to make each piece local, as I figure I'm the only one sharing the news about this town with the world, but also personal and universal—that way you don't have to live nearby to be interested. I spend more time on them than they are worth, but from the beginning I have felt an obligation to say something valuable. I looked to the Book of Common Prayer for guidance and found the prayer "For those who Influence Public Opinion." (It's an Episcopalian thing, these carefully scripted prayers for every possible need.) It says that those of us who write what "many read" (a writer can hope this is true) need to do our part "in making the heart of this people wise, its mind sound, and its will righteous." It sounds corny, and I know I miss the ball more than I hit it out of the park, but at least I'm swinging for the fences. I still say that prayer before I begin every column. Blessing words, like blessing boats, can't hurt. It may even help.

Anyway, I missed only one column in the year I was recovering from my accident, and that was the first one after the surgery. My deadline is Tuesday. (Well, actually it is the end of the day Monday, but I have learned that no one edits it until midday Tuesday, but that is another story.) I was hit on a Thursday, operated on on a Friday, and was still in and out of consciousness that next Tuesday. I made

the following deadline and every one after that. Those
columns were all about the shock, grief, anger, and even
small joys that come with such a life-changing experience. I also shared my mother's illness and death with my
readers. Describing events, articulating my feelings, and
making it all mean something was healing. My friends
and neighbors don't have the forum I do for the big stories
of their lives. Maybe that's why the pastors and priest are
reading all these names of the dead now, I thought, and
why the people who loved and lost them want them to,
and why they keep walking right up in front of everyone
to drop a flower in that basket and then walk back, facing us all with solemn, often wet faces. This is my story,
they seem to say, and this is why I am the way I am. For
myself, it's why those kids smoking on Main Street make
me so mad or why I cry at the school Christmas concert
every year or why I forgot about last week's library board
meeting. I am broken, too, and I have some stuff on my
mind so please be kind to me, which is a long way of saying that sharing grief does help.

Then I heard Olen Nash's name. I watched as his
mother, my friend Becky, walked up with a flower to put
in the basket. Her husband, Don, was already out trolling
for king salmon in his new boat. My son, Christian—he's
almost eighteen—will join him as a deckhand as soon as
school is out in May. They are both looking forward to
it. It has been seven years since Olen dove off the back
of the Nashes' sinking fifty-four-foot commercial fishing

boat, the *Becca Dawn,* toward a life raft he hoped would save him and his brothers and a friend. He was the only one who didn't survive.

Before she reached the basket with her flower, Becky's face crumpled and she pivoted back into the parting crowd. I intercepted her, linked her arm around mine, and we kept right on walking—away from everyone, toward Lookout Park, while the bell rang and more names were read. It was warmer with the wind at our backs. Soon we were snuffling and then sobbing. Once we were out of earshot, we stopped and had a pretty good cry. It was such a mess, this remembering, so good and so bad at the same time. We were both so snotty and wet that we started laughing.

"You sure you want Christian to fish with Don?" Becky asked, wiping her nose with a mitten.

I wiped mine on my sleeve and said sure I did. "Besides, he could just as easily be run over by a truck."

Which made us laugh some more.

Becky wanted to drop the flower near Olen's plaque on the Fishermen's Memorial, and so we started to climb up over the rotting snow berm, but the sun had softened it and we sank to our thighs. "Oh, what the heck," Becky said, chucking the stiff pink carnation up and over the dirty snow pile. Then she said, "Let's get out of here. I've had enough."

. . .

THAT NIGHT THE NORTHERN lights flashed and swirled above the roof of our weathered shingle home near where the Chilkat River meets the sea. Some of the white, swooping, teardrop-shaped lights tumbled like ghosts. Others spun in colorful hurricane swirls with long blue, green, and pink ribbons trailing off into the navy blue night. One golden banner above Mt. Ripinsky moved up and down in an electrocardiogram way, graphing the beating of so many hearts. I had never seen a light show like it. My husband, Chip, came out to look, too, and we called the kids: our teenagers Christian, J.J., and Stoli. (Our older daughters Sarah and Eliza were away; one at college, the other working at a ski resort in Utah.) By the time everyone made it outside the show was all over, without a hint of what had been there. Nothing remained except the stars shyly blinking. It was cold again; no doubt we'd have at least one more frost. I had on a down coat so, as the rest of my family went back inside, I stayed out a little longer, all by myself, standing in the gravel drive, looking up, watching and waiting.

The stars expanded and contracted. I thought I saw a shooting star, but it may have been a satellite. I wished I knew more about the night sky. I wished I knew more about a lot of things. At the Blessing of the Fleet, the Men of Note also sang the old verse "Grant us wisdom, grant us courage / For the living of these days / For the living of these days." At the end of a gentle, not cruel, April day, a day so full of joy and sorrow, to ask for a little wisdom and a little courage seemed reasonable and possible. The best kind of prayer. "What the heck," as Becky would say, why not ask? It can't hurt.

So I did, humming ever so softly to whoever might be listening.

CHAPTER 2

Be Still My Praying Feet

O God, make speed to save us.
O Lord, make haste to help us.
—Book of Common Prayer

Writing Wilma Henderson's obituary I learned that the very proper and always formidable farmwife and Presbyterian elder kept a copy of an African proverb, "Pray with your feet," as a bookmark in her Bible. This was not a surprise. Wilma was a doer. She was dedicated to her farm, to her family, and, above all, to community improvement, from sprucing up parks with flowers to organizing the annual school spelling bee. She taught God's word in Sunday school and made sure children (and adults) used correct grammar to explain it. Her grown daughters told me that she circled mistakes in their letters from college and returned them. "And we were good students!" one said. When Wilma was the volunteer librarian, back before we paid library staff, she would collect overdue books in person. In town, when she spied an improperly parked vehicle, say, in front of a fire hydrant or blocking a crosswalk, she would track down the owner in the grocery store or a café and ask him or her to move it, while she watched.

The problem with linking action to faith is that it requires a sturdy body. Once Wilma's broke down, she took to her bed and never got up again. She was eighty-nine years old when she died in the front room of her little old farmhouse. Her family didn't know what the cause of death was. She had always been ramrod fit—she was a great walker—and had rarely been to the doctor. For the obituary her family asked me to report that she died of natural causes, which, of course, my editor, Tom, wouldn't allow. After a few phone calls and Tom's chat with Wilma's husband, the former borough mayor, who explained that his wife didn't want to see a doctor or be sent to Juneau for tests—she never liked hospitals and already knew she was dying and didn't need to know what from—Tom had no choice but to let me write that she died of old age. I even quoted her husband's ironically ungrammatical explanation, "She just wore out."

Like Wilma, I think of myself as an active prayer. My faith has never been about what I feel; it is about what I do. Although—and here's the concern about even wading into this whole tricky discussion—this is not to imply in any way that I always do what's right, or that I even know what the right thing is half of the time. Not only do I *not* have the answers to, as Garrison Keillor's alter ego private eye Guy Noir would say, "life's persistent questions," I'm not even sure what the questions are. But I have learned something about life and death and faith from living in a small town, from writing obituaries, and from my own near miss. Anyway, to complement my action philosophy, I have always prayed before I go to sleep, for the same reason I floss my teeth: it's a good habit. I say the Our Father (who art in heaven, hallowed be thy Name . . .) as a kind of password, then I ask God to please bless a fairly long list of family, friends, and neighbors, and then I thank Him (or maybe Her?) for all my blessings, my family, our home, and this community, and then I wrap it up with general pleas for action on the big issues facing humanity: war, peace, poverty, and global warming—the issues and events that I don't have much control over.

Then I was run over by a truck and lost control of just about everything. I was flown out of town, put back together, hospitalized, and finally placed in a nursing home a thousand miles away from home until I was strong enough to travel—in other words, until I was able to sit up in the wheelchair (or airplane seat) for at least four hours. In Seattle, Dr. Chip Routt explained that I should train for this the same way I used to train for marathons, gradually increasing minutes sitting up just as I once increased miles running. It took a week before I was strong enough to be transferred from the bed to the wheelchair and back, and the effort of lifting and sliding and holding up my braced pelvis was exhausting. At the end of the day (and the beginning and middle), the only act I could do without physical pain was praying, but I had to learn how to do it differently. I couldn't pray with my feet so I had to pray with something else.

Luckily I didn't have far to look for guidance. I am an Episcopalian, and we have a whole textbook of prayers: the ancient (well, 1549) and little-modified Book of Common Prayer. It is divided up into helpful sections, Morning, Noonday, and Evening prayer for what are called the Daily Offices for home or church, as well as special services for big events such as baptism, marriage, and burial. There is even a whole section of additional prayers for just about every occasion and human condition. A rarely used and old-fashioned service called Compline ends the Episcopal Church day, usually around ten at night. Friends from St. Michael and All Angels, the tiny mission church I attend on Sunday mornings in the lobby of the Chilkat Center for the Arts, sent me a CD of a sung and chanted version of Compline recorded at St. Mark's Cathedral right in Seattle. Compline is the shortest of the Daily Offices and has fewer changeable parts (readings and prayers); it is meant to be a gentle, easy-to-recite, and comforting close to the day.

I loved the simple melodies and notes of the plainsong, but I also loved the words. My favorite Compline prayer, which fit so well with my circumstance, especially as the night shift came on in the nursing home, was:

Keep watch, dear Lord, with those who work, or watch, or weep this night, and give your angels charge over those who sleep. Tend the sick, Lord Christ; give rest to the weary, bless the dying, soothe the suffering, pity the afflicted, shield the joyous; and all for your love's sake. Amen.

"Shield the joyous" is poetry. I was so far from joyful, yet I was praying for that and I knew what it meant. I had been filled with joy just before Kevin's truck hit me. I had been glowing with the joy of my imagined success. My first book was coming out soon, and I was fantasizing about doing what glamorous real writers might do. Just thinking about that now makes me flush with embarrassment. There's that, and I have teenagers so I know heartache and sometimes-bad choices can spring from great joy. The way "shield the joyous" was tucked in there with all that care and suffering (which pretty much summed up what was going on all around me) helped reinforce what I already knew: that you can't have real joy if you don't understand what real sorrow is.

I had never seen woe like this, so I was even more appreciative of the life I had led before my accident and more determined to gain at least some of it back. This was what the stage manager in *Our Town* called a vicious circle. You have to love life to live life, he said, and because we love it, losing a part of it—a favorite person or place or even your ability to do the chores you used to—is so painful. I had to learn how to lose a little control, a little pride, without losing it all. I had to learn to love the people around me enough to let them pray with their feet. As nutty or "woo-woo" as it may sound, I had to let go to hold on.

The Vietnamese Buddhist monk Thich Nhat Hanh tells a story about a man stranded on a mountain (he can't go up or down) and of another man at an intersection (he is so confused he doesn't know which way to turn). Both are equally stuck, and the worst choice either man can make is trying to think and plan his way out of it. The only way out of a bad situation for them—and, by extension, for all of us—advises the good monk, is to "surrender to the moment" and not even pretend to know the way out. As Bob Dylan sings, "Don't think twice, it's all right."

The truck hitting me was bad, but the place I call the "Sleepless in Seattle Nursing Home" was worse. As nursing homes go, I suppose it was a fine one, but even the best nursing homes are places you don't want to be. (This is not good news because the fastest growing segment of the U.S. population is eighty-five and older, and it will be that way for at least the next thirty years. We need to fix this system for our grandparents, parents, and ourselves. That's fodder for a newspaper column, or three.)

I had to go to the nursing home because I was too weak and busted up to fly on a commercial jet to Juneau and then take a four-and-a-half-hour ferry ride home to Haines (population about 2,400). There is no road in or out of Juneau, Alaska's capital and the nearest city to Haines.

The only access is by sea or air. The Haines airport is too small to have jet service, and I couldn't climb into a small plane. Also, with the extent of my fractures there was a risk that the experimental external brace might not repair them, so the doctors wanted me close to a hospital—and there is no hospital in Haines. In short, I was in the same fix as the guy on the mountain and the guy at the crossroads. There was nothing to do but stay.

I had imagined that I would be rehabbing in a residential wing of some place that was used by, say, the Seattle Seahawks as a training center, a health club–type facility full of athletes and trainers. I had imagined wood-floored studios, massage tables, whirlpool tubs, acupuncture treatments, yoga classes, spinning bikes in a glass-walled room overlooking Puget Sound, and a dining service that offered fresh salmon, whole grain breads, and fruit smoothies loaded with vitamins and minerals. My roommate would be a skier, someone like Picabo Street, recovering from another broken leg, or an equestrian with a plaster-encased foot up in the air and an arm in a sling blaming it on a "skittish mare" and swearing in a British accent.

When the ambulance transporting me from the hospital pulled up outside the Sleepless in Seattle Nursing Home, I was lying on my back (as I would be for most of the next twelve weeks), but I could see the tops of dogwood trees blooming. The light-filled entry was full of hanging plants, and I heard a bubbling fish tank. As they wheeled my gurney through the commons area, though, I didn't see strong men and women on crutches. From the corner of my eyes, I saw old people in wheelchairs. Very old people. They were slumped over, sleeping, turning in slow circles, or muttering to themselves. They were all ancient and ill, and not in a temporary kind of way. These people did not have torn rotator cuffs or ruptured cruciate ligaments. They were "wore out," just like Wilma had been. They would be leaving here only in a hearse. How right Wilma was to stay home in her own bed rather than, as my golfing mother would have said, playing out the back nine of her life in a place like this. I don't mean to say there wasn't any joy, but it was a hard, sad place. Later, in the physical therapy room, I would meet one tweedy old gentleman in hiking shoes who came daily to rub the side of his stroke-stricken wife's face; she was unable to speak or move. They'd been married sixty years, he would tell me. Watching them then I was grateful that I was on the mend and that Chip would not be caring for me that way for the rest of our lives. Chip said he understood why the husband came by each day, and then he reminded me, as he had daily since the accident, that so many people had it harder than we did. He had come with me on the medevac flight and stayed the entire time I was in Seattle.

The attendants wheeled me past these ghosts of Christmas future into the doorway of a long, narrow room with a window down at one end. That end was occupied by an old woman and as much "stuff" from her former home as possible: a wood-console TV, plaid recliner, end tables, lamps, a rug, framed pictures of children and grandchildren, and pots of plastic plants were all wedged in tight. Although it was April, there was an artificial Christmas tree with blinking colored lights next to the hospital bed, which was occupied by Nadine. She was seventy-five years old and had lived in this room for three years.

To heal I knew I needed to have sunlight and fresh air. Vitamin D promotes calcium absorption, and calcium makes bone, and I needed plenty of that. I also needed crisp vegetables and soft cotton sheets. I had been hoping for organic kale soups and healing touch therapy. That was looking less and less likely. I knew right away that I would never get anywhere near that window, and I was just as sure that Nadine would never willingly open it.

Dylan Thomas would have approved of what happened next, but no one else would. I did not go gently into that not-so-good room. I lay on that stretcher and pitched as much of a fit as an immobile, sedated person can. I yelled at Chip to do something. I said I wasn't staying here, that there must be a better place. The private ambulance company crew chief said he had other patients to transport and that they needed to pick me up now and put me in the bed in Nadine's room and take their gurney back. I said I wasn't staying, that this was not my room, or my nursing home, that there had been a big mistake. There must be a different, more rehabby place for me to go to. He said there wasn't, that this was where they were supposed to drop me off. He checked his orders, flipping the papers on his clipboard. Then he sighed and said, firmly, that I couldn't go back to the hospital, I couldn't go home, and I couldn't go to a hotel room. I couldn't even sit up in a chair, much less a cab.

Well, shit.

I had been so brave until that moment; I really had been. In the hospital, after the surgery, alone with the machines beeping and blinking, I had cried only a little, even after a doctor friend from Juneau had called to tell me I'd be in pain for the rest of my life and should be happy if I could walk again, much less run, hike, or ride a bike. "You are a very lucky woman," he said, "but this is the real deal, a life-changing event that you will never recover fully from." Even then, I had been upbeat in my response to him and with my own thoughts, too, there in the dark as the rain ran down the big window and another ambulance pulled into the emergency room, bearing with it another lucky person who would be saved and mended and then sent gratefully on her way, like me. That was what I was thinking then. This was what I was thinking now: I suddenly felt so helpless, so sad, so busted up and frail—so alone in this body of mine that wouldn't work anymore that I was dizzy with grief. This was really unfair. I had done nothing to deserve it. I covered my face with my hands and sobbed. It felt like my heart was breaking. I wondered if I could die from this kind of hopelessness. If I did, would it be natural causes? Tom would probably insist that in my obit it be attributed to "complications from trauma and pelvic surgery."

Then I looked up and saw Chip's red-rimmed eyes and stricken face and knew I had to stop crying and stop complaining.

I still felt like I had a leaking hole in my heart, but I decided to quit sharing that news with the people who cared about me. I prayed. I prayed for help. I began like I always had, "Our Father, who art in heaven . . ." and just said all the words. Nothing happened. So I tried it the way I'd read St. Ignatius had, and took one full breath for each word. It was like yoga and a prayer. I felt better. I felt safer. I understood what a born-again Christian neighbor meant when she wrote she'd been praying for God to hold me in the palm of His hand. I have coached high school runners for fifteen years, and I knew from experience that if you practice an action or repeat a thought enough, it will transform you. I'd received a card from one of my runners, who wrote, "Walk it off, Heather." He made me laugh. How many times had I looked at hurting young athletes and given them that same advice? It was time to practice what I coached. If I acted positive, if I said the right things often enough, then I should start to believe them, and, maybe, heal. I knew all that, but I also kept hearing one of the singer-songwriters I always play when I volunteer on the radio, Texan Nanci Griffith, singing "If wishes were changes we'd all live in roses" and children would never cry in their sleep.

I let the ambulance crew lift me into the bed, and I lay there with my eyes squeezed shut while Chip left to speak with the nursing home manager. She promised I'd have my own room with a window by Monday. It was Friday. After Chip had held my hand, after my heart had stopped beating funny, after I had promised him and myself I'd be a good sport, we called home. I told the kids I had a sunny room with a nice view, that the nursing home was great, and that I'd been popping wheelies in my new wheelchair. I said I was feeling much better and would be home as soon as they let me out, which could be any day. I said "I love you" to each of them and that I'd call tomorrow. Everything except the last part was a lie.

Mario Juarez, an old friend who used to live in Haines and who had been with us daily since we arrived in Seattle, found Chip a place to stay, an empty apartment that was between buyers. There was a mattress, and he loaned Chip a sleeping bag. It had been a long day. Chip was tired. He kissed my forehead and headed "home," saying he'd see me first thing in the morning.

I prayed I'd live that long.

MY ROOMMATE NADINE sang a lot. Her favorite song was the one about Johnny being too long at the fair, punctuated with "Oh my Lord, I forgot the words." Luckily she didn't sing all night. Nadine was one of the few residents who slept. She even slept through the midnight fire alarm. She slept through the sirens and lights and rumbling emergency rigs pulling into the parking lot one floor below us. To be on the second floor of a nursing home and hear alarms and sirens and see red and blue lights flashing against the ceiling and walls and know that you cannot even transfer yourself into a wheelchair, much less move anywhere in it, makes any other fear trivial. I was stuck there as fire doors slammed shut, smoke alarms blared, old people screamed, and all but the emergency lights went out.

"Help," I yelled, but no one came. "Help," I yelled louder. "Help, Help, Help!" I screamed, and no one came. I did wake Nadine, though, who coughed and said, "Oh, honey, it's only a drill."

A drill? At this hour? I mean, honestly, how cruel and unkind is that? What were they thinking? Who runs this place? Nadine said they do it at night because the firemen don't have much else to do, so they bring the trucks and practice putting up their ladders.

There were no intercoms, or else my cry for help would have been broadcast around the building. Instead, we had to squeeze a rubber ball that turned on a light outside the door of our room. When a nurse or aide saw it, he or she would come and help with a bedpan or glass of water or pain pills, sooner or, mostly, later. The seasoned residents quit squeezing the ball and hollered when they wanted attention. When Nadine had an accident in the night, she yelled until Sebele, a nurse's aide, came. Sebele, like most of the staff, was African. She was from Eritrea. She didn't speak English well, but she did understand the language of her patients. She treated Nadine gently. She changed her bed at two in the morning and cleaned Nadine as if she were wiping up a toddler—as if it were no more unusual and no more of a mess and no more of an odor—before helping her into clean pajamas.

Maria was the day nurse. She was from the Philippines and had a home in Seattle and another near Manila. She teased Nadine, who had that cranky way about her old people can acquire. When Nadine wanted Maria to change the channel on the TV, Maria made Nadine do it herself. Not in a mean way, but because she wanted Nadine to do whatever she was still able to do. Maria made me feel so safe, I took a nap.

The head aide was Tekla. (I'm not sure how to spell this or any of the African names, and I never did learn any of the nurses' or aides' last names.) When I asked where he was from, he said, "Seattle," in a thick accent. When I asked him again, he said, "Africa." He was from Eritrea, too. I didn't want him helping with my bedpan. I requested that he find a woman to do it. "Where's Sebele?" She was busy, he said. But his eyes said what he was thinking. They said I didn't trust him because he was a big black man from Africa who couldn't speak English very well. I was embarrassed, because that is what I had been thinking. So much for letting go, for surrendering, for really grasping the point of the Lord's Prayer.

Oh, God, forgive me my trespasses.

Not to excuse the unforgivable, but I was in a pretty

vulnerable position. I didn't want a strange, foreign man lifting up my nightgown and setting my bare bottom on a bedpan, waiting until I went, and then cleaning me up with rubber gloves and baby wipes. I was scared and humiliated and I couldn't help it.

Tekla told me that he understood my modesty but that, if I had to go to the bathroom and a woman couldn't be found in time, it would be better to have him help me than to soil myself. That was his word, soil. I didn't want to wet the bed. When you have so little control over what is happening, you make deals with yourself. My first one was that I would never join the tragic Greek chorus of "helps" echoing along the corridors in the night. So much for that. But my second personal goal was that I would never wet the bed. I never did. That meant I had to let strangers—some men, some women, some black, some white, some young, some old—help me do what I never thought anyone but me would do. Later, once I had become more used to Tekla and he had given me shots and pills, changed my bed, cleaned my wounds and everywhere else, all of it, I told him I thought he must have been a doctor back in Eritrea. This time his eyes said, "Thank you." They were all so good to me, these saints of Seattle, that I still can't believe it. I have begun to pay them back, in a karmic kind of way, as a Hospice of Haines volunteer.

What you need to know now is that it had been a very long weekend in the Sleepless in Seattle Nursing Home, and it was about to become longer. Sunday night, after

Chip went home, the lady in the room next door wailed, "Help me." Soon, everyone on the hall joined her in wailing "Help" and "Help me." One missed her house; another missed her daughter; one man couldn't say what was wrong, but he took off all his clothes and begged for someone to call him a cab. The red-haired Mormon girl who was volunteering in the home as part of her premed gerontology class ran after him gently calling, "Naked man, naked man, oh, naked man, please stop." Nadine woke up angry and yelled for them all to be quiet. When that didn't work she sighed, "Lord have mercy" and sang about Johnny and the fair until she dozed off.

My new room wasn't ready until Wednesday. It should have been a big day for me. The first copy of my book arrived. I shouted to Nadine that I had written a book. She was hard of hearing so I held it up for her to see. "Is it large print?" she asked. I said no.

"Do they have it on tape?" I said I didn't think so. "What good is it then?" she asked.

Not much, I guess. Funny how I thought writing a book would change my life. Be careful what you wish for.

The new room was on a different floor. Chip went down and checked it out and said it was bigger and there was a nice window. Maria came and gave me my medication and said it was nice to have known me. Turns out each floor had its own staff. Tekla brought the lunch tray and explained that I'd have different nurses and different aides and even a different guy mopping the floor. He also said that no matter what I was promised, he wouldn't be surprised if I was assigned another roommate. More old people are dropped off each day, he said.

And so, after everything, I decided to stay where I was.

That evening, before we went to sleep, I asked Nadine if she liked her life at the Sleepless in Seattle Nursing Home. "Well," she sighed, "it's clean, and I'm not alone. That's the main thing. I'm not alone."

I put on my headphones and said goodnight. Before turning on the Compline CD, I had a conversation with the feeling I think might be God or the Holy Spirit or that so-called still, small voice I've heard sometimes speaks to those who want to hear it but who was, I was learning, the friend to whom I could whine, the one to whom I could tell how lonely I was. The one I could admit to what I wouldn't let anyone else know. The one I didn't have to be brave for. I told Her (it was easier having this wise friend be female) that I couldn't feel my right leg and might never be able to and that I was worried about suffering a heart-stopping blood clot. I said I wanted to see my children so badly. I wanted to be able to run again. I really wanted a hot shower. I was hungry but so constipated from the morphine, I was afraid to eat. There in that holy darkness, even though Chip was not with me and my children were a thousand miles away, I wasn't alone anymore. (And I'm not talking about Nadine, bless her snoring heart.) Someone who loved me was listening and watching over me.

I didn't ever hear Her speak to me, but I knew She was there. I fell asleep to the comforting rhythms of the now-familiar prayers and music of Compline. I wasn't praying with my feet. I wasn't doing anything at all. I felt better than I had since my accident.

AFTER WILMA HENDERSON DIED, her pastor, my friend Ron Horn from the Presbyterian church, told me that in her last weeks and especially her last days she had visibly softened. That the Holy Spirit had gentled her. I bet she learned to pray lying down, too. I bet that after a lifetime of good works, she discovered that sometimes the best thing a strong woman can do is nothing. Nothing at all.

I spent three weeks in the nursing home. The farther away I got from those early days of recovery, the less I sought solace in that prayerful stillness and the less I listened to Compline, that last service of the day. And I suppose this is typical. I didn't need either as much, and other thoughts began filling my days and my nights again.

But I still pray before sleep, even if it is just the Our Father and the thank-yous. It feels different now, more intimate. The other night when I finished my prayers, I looked out the window at the gray, rainy, starless sky outside my bedroom window, and I felt a heavy ache, like homesickness almost, even though I was tucked in my own bed, in my favorite place in the whole world. It was not a pang for me this time or for my friends and family.

I've been reading, listening, and watching the news. There is so much grief in the world I sometimes don't know how it keeps spinning. "Our Father," I began, breathing with each word and, when I was done, God and I talked, or I talked and He listened. I can't say we changed anything, but I can't say we didn't, either.

CHAPTER 3

You Do Not Know

*Watch, for you do not know when the master of the
house will come, in the evening, or at midnight or
at cock crow.* —Mark 13:35

I said I'd tell you more about my accident and I will.
But first I want to share a couple of uncanny occurrences that happened before I was run over — instruc-
tional moments that I don't think were just coincidences.
If this were a novel, they would be considered heavy
foreshadowing.

Here's the first one. I had been spring-cleaning like
crazy: washing all the windows, inside and out, hauling
bags full of clothes to the Salvation Army, airing blankets,
dusting bookshelves, and scrubbing floors. I even mucked
out and hosed down the chicken coop, making it all fresh
and clean.

Then I decided to move our bedroom up to the third
floor, so that Chip and I could have our own bathroom.

This used to be our older daughters' attic sanctuary, but they were both in college now and could share our old room on the second floor when they were home for the summer or Christmas vacation. I made Sarah's tiny room our closet and filled up Eliza's cozy room with our bed and night tables. It's small and tucked under the eaves but has a great window overlooking the Chilkat Inlet and the mountains. I decided to paint both rooms a deep blue to match the spring sky. I was on a ladder rolling the walls in the bedroom when the Safety Report came on the radio.

Fireman Al Badgley and volunteer Travis Reid were giving the weekly talk. And, yes, he is really called Fireman Al. Officially he's the training officer for the volunteer fire department, but he's really the guy who responds to just about every ambulance call. There were "250 on the nose" last year, according to Al. The only time Al doesn't go on a call is when he's out of town on vacation or fishing too far from the dock. I have seen him leave his pew in the middle of a prayer, walk out during a commencement speech at a high school graduation, and drop his burger, grab his jacket, and leave his family at the Elks Club weekly hamburger feed. He's even left a funeral where he was supposed to be a pallbearer. Some days he has many calls: 3 a.m. (a young woman has been cut in a drunken fight with her boyfriend); 1 p.m. (a boy has broken his wrist playing basketball in gym class); 5 p.m. (a woman has slipped on the ice in front of the grocery store and hit her head); 7 p.m. (an elderly man thinks he's having a heart attack). Every single one of these people is better off because Al was there, speaking in his soft, ever-so-slightly-goofy Texas way, competently assessing the situation and directing the crew.

Al's wife is the choir director at the Presbyterian church. They have a son and a daughter, and his widowed mother comes up from Texas and stays with them every summer. When he's not on an ambulance call or at the fire hall, Al likes to fish and hunt. He celebrated his fiftieth birthday a few years back with a Sunday afternoon potluck picnic at the church. Built like a wiry cowboy, he just about always wears dark blue work pants, a matching shirt, and leather work boots. He has a bushy mustache, and his wife cuts his fly-away brown hair. At the annual lighting of the library Christmas tree this year, a little girl walked up to Al, who was sitting down nibbling on a plate of home-made cookies, sushi, and cheese and crackers from the potluck spread. He had already saved the day when an au-dio speaker from the PA system fell off the wall—luckily it missed hitting our dear elder Maisie Jones, but it nicked a boy kneeling next to Maisie's chair. Al stemmed the bleeding, opened the library first aid kit, and applied a butterfly bandage to the boy's forehead. He assured ev-eryone the child was okay, and the ceremony continued with a reading of the fire scene from *A Child's Christmas in Wales*. (The one in which they throw snowballs into the steamy house and the tiny old aunt asks the firemen if they'd like anything to read. I am not making this up; I was the reader.) But back to my story. Al was eating, and this solemn, blonde-haired little girl—Sally Chapell is her name—said, "I know you, you're Fireman Al." And he said, "Yes, I am." Then she said, "You help people." And he said, "I do my best." And then she asked him if he would fix her shoe, because the strap on her Mary Janes had come unbuckled. Al pulled her up onto his lap and fastened it.

NOW, IN MY drop-cloth-draped spring bedroom, Al and Travis were still talking on the radio, keeping me company and reminding drivers to watch for pedestrians and cyclists since more people were out enjoying the warm spring weather. "Most accidents occur within a mile of home," Al was saying. Then he warned that if someone does get hurt, if there's a "not-so-great situation" with "a person on the ground, or some such scenario," be sure not to move that person. Travis, who is a river-rafting guide and younger and hipper than Al, jumped in and told us to be sure to identify someone specific who will call 911. "Look right at him or her and say, 'Yo, dude, call 911,' and tell the dispatcher where you are, what's going on, and give them as many details as you possibly can to prepare the ambulance crew."

We sometimes call the Safety Report the Duh Report at our house because, with all due respect to Al, what person doesn't know not to set up a Christmas tree next to the woodstove? On the other hand, the lessons Al has taught our community about fire safety have kept Haines relatively blaze-free for twenty years. Al became a fireman after accidentally burning down his parents' cabin. No one was hurt, but the log home was reduced to coals. You could say he's been on a mission ever since to prevent that from happening to some other college kid. He also has greatly increased the expertise of the volunteer ambulance crew. Al, like me, the obituary writer, is part of the local death beat that works together when someone dies. Haines doesn't have a funeral parlor, so it's Al who brings the ambulance that is also the hearse and who asks members of the ambulance crew to help him pick up the body. And it's Al who often helps other volunteers prepare the body for burial. Al even watches over the corpse, as the morgue is in a garage at the fire hall where he works.

Fireman Al had played a big part in a near-death-experience story I'd been working on recently for the *Chilkat Valley News*. Gladys Meacock had survived a bizarre and enlightening occurrence the previous summer and after months of rehabilitation was finally back home and able to talk about it. The day Gladys almost died was just about perfect. Her orchard was loaded with cherries, and her husband, George, was mowing the big field behind the house. Above him eagles glided in the thermals in the shadow of Mt. Ripinsky. Across the bluff from the Meacock homestead, silver salmon swam up the Chilkat River. It was an idyllic Alaskan scene. All that was missing was a cow moose and her calf. It wasn't the kind of morning you'd think anything bad could happen—not that anyone could expect to be almost killed hanging laundry on the line.

One minute Gladys had been pinning up a rug, the next she was on the ground, unable to move her arms and legs. She had broken her neck. There are more than a few folks around here who, on a brightly polished day like the one Gladys almost died on, would look around and think that if they had to make the choice right then between their backyard and heaven, they'd stay put. So it is not that surprising that Gladys felt the same way, even after glimpsing what she is sure were the Elysian Fields.

Gladys is a retired science teacher in her early seventies who spent most of her career working in a juvenile detention facility in Anchorage. Gladys's heart knows something mystical happened that day, but the science teacher in her thinks that the tingly out-of-body sensation she experienced may be the result of "a visual brain pattern triggered by the severe trauma."

The Meacocks' clothesline had been made for Gladys's by-then-deceased mother-in-law, Mary. It was a wire cable strung between a pole in the ground and another pole on a small platform four steps up. The raised line kept the bottom of the sheets out of the snow in the winter and looked a bit like a dock on a sea of grass in the summer. Gladys was standing up there securing a heavy rug when the cable apparently snapped, from wear or weight no one is really sure, and rather than let go of it, Gladys reflexively grabbed on tight and, as she said, "became the whip end of a lashing cable." At first her husband and the EMTs thought she had tripped and fallen off the platform. But that didn't explain how she was so badly hurt. It just wasn't that far to drop.

Strangely, Gladys woke up on the warm lawn and felt wonderful, better than she ever had; she was wrapped in a blanket of bliss. "I had no thought of anything or anybody," she said, "and there was this strange orange-golden light." Gladys is not prone to fancy, but on this day she heard—very clearly—a voice, a voice that she is sure belonged to the ghost of her mother-in-law, Mary, another strong-armed and clear-headed Meacock woman, who never would have stood for Gladys being killed by her old clothesline, in her old backyard. "I heard Mary clear as day. 'Breathe,' she said. 'Breathe in and breathe out.'" So Gladys sucked in some air and exhaled more, and the magic feeling left, replaced by a barge-load of pain and fear. "I knew right then this would be my darkest hour," Gladys said, deepening her voice, leaning in, and opening her big blue Eskimo eyes extra wide.

Her husband called 911 and Fireman Al arrived. Gladys thinks the most important decision Al made was to believe her when she said she couldn't move and that it hurt terribly. And even though it was a lovely day and there was no real explanation at the time for what had happened, he treated her as if she had a serious spine injury, the kind people incur in car accidents or falling off roofs.

Gladys told me that she believes part of the reason she didn't die and wasn't paralyzed was that she stayed alert and communicated what she was feeling and thinking to Al and his crew. She never quit talking, even though it hurt so much that she was tempted to just close her eyes, but she really did not want to die that way, on that day, right then. Gladys was not ready to shed her mortal coil just yet.

I thought about all this as I stood on the ladder painting my room. Al was still talking on the radio. He'd moved on to the hazards of spring boating: "You can't always predict what the weather will do. A nice calm day can change fast, so wear a life jacket and bring extra fuel and some means to make the boat go if the engine quits—an oar or what have you." Travis chimed in with, "You definitely don't want to get yourself up a you-know-what creek without a paddle. Like the scouts say, be prepared."

Or like Mark's Gospel says, "You do not know when the master of the house will come." We don't know when God will tap us on the shoulder and say, "Time's up." So watch, pay attention, and, as Pastor Ron Horn said at Wilma Henderson's funeral, "Do good."

I HAD MUCH MORE on my mind a few days later, on the first real spring day of the year, while I was riding my bike for the second time since the previous fall and mentally planning my first book tour, which would begin in six weeks in Boston and take me to Denver, Salt Lake

City, the Bay Area, Portland, Seattle, Bellingham, then up to Fairbanks, Anchorage, and down to Juneau before ending up back home in Haines. I wouldn't be in any town or city for more than two days. And I'd be alone.

I had never been gone from my children or my husband that long. I'm not a traveler. I get homesick in Juneau. I'm terrified of flying. Three of my next-door neighbors have died in small-plane crashes. I am even more afraid of big jets. They fly so high and fast that I can't imagine having to land on, say, a rock-free strip of beach or an old logging road if the weather closed in or an engine quit. So Dr. Feldman, or Len (I call him both—it's Dr. Feldman in the office and Len when he's out in his garden across the road from mine), gives me just enough Valium pills to take one for each leg of the trip whenever I must travel across the state or the country. (My extended family lives in New York, my in-laws are in Virginia and Florida.)

I might not like planes, but I love my bicycle. It is a Trek road bike made of carbon fiber and light enough to lift with two fingers. It is nicer than my old Subaru. Riding my bicycle fast may be as close as I'll come to finding that peace they promise in church, the one that passes all understanding. When I'm riding twenty miles an hour, with a tailwind, drafting behind another rider, I think it must be what nirvana feels like. And, it's good for me. Just dressing for the ride had given me pleasure. I had on my padded shorts, tights, warm jersey, helmet, gloves, and neon orange wind jacket. This was an easy

ride. It takes me a few outings each spring to become re-
acquainted with my pedaling muscles and with the skinny
seat. As I rode, I was thinking about all of the changes in
my life that the publication of my first book might bring.
I practiced answering imaginary questions from Oprah.
"Why," Oprah asks in my daydreaming head, "would
anyone be interested in the life of an obituary writer in
Haines, Alaska?" I think a minute, taking in the lights,
the couch, all those people, Oprah's imposing and successful self, and reply, "Uh, you know, I have no friggin'
idea." Cut to a commercial and my short, happy career as
an author is over.

I was breathing hard as I pedaled up Cemetery Hill.
I sat up tall going over the top, realizing that I couldn't
worry about an interview that would never happen. Instead, I had to plan how I was going to survive the trips
to bookstores, the readings, the travel. If I don't overcome
my fear of flying, I thought, I may not be able to even do
the tour. If I take drugs for each leg of the trip, I'll be
dopey the whole time. Also, what will I wear? If I am an
author now, then I should dress like one. Should I buy a
silk scarf? What would I do with it, toss it over my shoulder and pretend as if I always dress this way, like it's not a
costume in a play? Do women writers wear tweed jackets,
or are they only for men? I had bought new shoes, but
they were green running-style shoes. Green canvas. Pea
green canvas. Oh God, what was I thinking?

Thoreau was right when he said to be wary of anything

that requires new clothes, because that's what was on my mind as I glided down the otherwise empty, late-morning street, on a calm, clear, spring morning when the black pickup stopped at the intersection and its driver glanced quickly around and then pulled right out in front of me. He didn't hear my yells, so I turned toward a ditch, planning to copy Lance Armstrong when he avoided a pileup of wrecked riders in the Tour de France by cutting across a field.

Instead of guiding my bike as if it were a runaway horse across the grass and back up onto the pavement, then heading off to a stage victory and the first yellow jersey for a woman in the Tour de France, my tires skidded on sand left over from winter snowplows. I fell down with a pop, the sound my cycling shoes made as they came unclipped from the pedals, and the beautiful bike slipped out from under me and clattered away. Dragging my gloved hands on the road to slow myself down, I prayed I'd stop before I went under the truck. Please, God, don't let the wheel run over my head. I slid like that—sitting up, legs out, hands back, my whole body tense and flexed—right between the front and rear wheels. The back tire of the new king-cab, three-quarter-ton Chevy pickup rolled right over my lap. My face was inches from the bright chrome hubcap. I could have kissed the raised chevron. I felt a kind of wump and my abdomen, lower back, and upper legs suddenly hurt so bad that I couldn't breathe. Is this it? I thought. Am I going to die like this? I mean, whatever happened to women's intuition? Shouldn't I have some? I had just been—quite literally—run over by *a fucking truck,* and I didn't sense it coming at all. Maybe this is how it is with all deaths; maybe death catches us all by surprise. A year later, visiting my mother in her last hours, drained as she was from the chemotherapy, asleep and never waking, I kept looking at her one eyebrow, raised in a question mark.

You can't interview a dead person for her obituary. I have always wanted to meet a ghost, but none has ever appeared at the foot of my bed. Like most of us, I know only of near misses, nothing of what happens when all the lights go out on earth. Still, I thought, there had to be more to the end of my life than this. I waited a second. I was still alive. Kevin, the driver, ran toward me, calling my name. He's the manager of the big grocery store on Main Street. His girlfriend graduated from Haines High in my daughter's class. My friend Joanne charged off her nearby deck across the lawn toward us, her newest spaniel, a black cocker named Harry, barking after her. I had just waved hello to Joanne a moment earlier.

I was now down on the ground just as Gladys had been. I thought about her and Al and the lessons I'd learned so recently, and everything both sped up and moved very slowly. When my oldest daughter was in grade school, a state trooper spoke to her class. He said he had seen people die because they were afraid, because they thought they would die, and that he had seen people survive those same kinds of situations because they weren't afraid and didn't think they would die. He gave an example of a fellow trooper who was shot through a door he was knocking on. He was hit in the shoulder. It should not have been a life-threatening injury, but he died of the traumatic surprise. He thought the shot was fatal and so it became.

I wanted to live, and I made a deal with God. I'll take the wheelchair, if I can still move my arms. I don't want to live like Christopher Reeve had, but I could live like Dave Olerud. (I feel bad about not wanting to survive if it meant I'd be a quadriplegic, and I mean no disrespect to people who are, but that's how I felt when faced with the actual, painful possibility. It may be shameful to admit, but I don't believe I could live an immobile life; I am not strong enough.) Dave Olerud, a former schoolteacher and owner of the local sporting goods store, lost the use of his legs in a construction accident. He was putting up a wall during a happy community barn-raising-style event at the American Bald Eagle Foundation's natural history center when something went terribly wrong and the wall fell back on the volunteers. He was crushed underneath it.

Today Dave is another part of the puzzle of my survival. I remembered that he didn't just close his eyes and die. He hadn't, so I wouldn't. Same with Gladys. Even now, looking back on all of this almost four years later, my chagrin has not faded over the irony of my column running in that day's *Anchorage Daily News*—the one that people across Alaska were reading as I lay in the road bleeding—being headlined "Matters of Life and Death." I mean, it's really pretty funny, when you think about it. The column was all about Gladys surviving her broken neck and a fisherman who fell through the ice while clamming and saw a bright light as well.

Unlike those two, I could see clearly. No flashes of heaven blinded me. Peace didn't blanket me, and I didn't feel any warm glow. I didn't want to. I willfully stayed, as my friend and fellow Hospice of Haines volunteer Beth MacCready would say, "present." (Beth practices Eastern-style meditation in a hut she built for this purpose on the beach.) I didn't even close my eyes, in case they wouldn't reopen. I prayed, whispering fast, to make sure my message arrived there in time: "Hail Mary, full of grace, the Lord is with thee, blessed art thou among women and blessed is the fruit of thy womb, Jesus Christ. Holy Mary, mother of God, pray for us sinners now and at the hour of our death, Amen." I said it the right way. Usually I modify the Hail Mary with "pray for us now, and in the hour of our need," omitting the sinning and death parts because they seem so melodramatic. Not that day. Heeding a lesson from my interview with Gladys, I told Kevin not to touch me—he might make things worse—and, remembering the instructions from the radio's Safety Report, I looked right into Joanne's light eyes and said, "Joanne, dial 911 and tell Al that Heather's been hit by a car." I did not see (or hear) any angel choirs flying close to the ground, but I did see Dave Olerud spinning his wheelchair with a laughing grandchild on his lap. Please, I prayed, let me have that much.

(Before I go on, there is one more thing you need to know. Kevin wasn't drunk or speeding or doing anything reckless. He just didn't see me. He wasn't paying that close attention. It could have been any one of us behind the wheel. It could have been me or you driving that truck.)

Three months later, after I was well enough to have Travis and Fireman Al and the other volunteer EMTs who responded to the call over to the house for a thank-you potluck, they said that they still couldn't believe I had been run over and was able to speak to them and explain the circumstances. Travis, who is usually glib and breezy, teared up when he saw me. He said he was grateful I had survived. He hadn't thought I would. Back then I didn't want to know more; I was still too busy recovering to worry about what might have happened the day of the accident. But recently I asked Travis to explain why he thought I kept talking and appeared to be better off than I was. I had hoped he'd say it might be a miracle or that I was extra brave. Instead he said, "It's simple: you were in shock." Then he said, "Shit, Heather, you should have been dead. You had tire tracks on your abdomen and you were talking about how you hadn't shaved your legs. It was real, real bad. People die of broken pelvises all the time. If we hadn't been there so fast, if you had been alone, and it had taken any longer to reach you, or get you to Seattle, your pelvic girdle would have collapsed on itself, closing blood vessels, crushing nerves, puncturing—you'd basically bleed out." He may have noticed the look of horror on my face, because then he said, more gently, that there was one thing that had been in my favor.

"Faith?" I asked.

"No, I don't know about that," he said (unlike Al, Travis is not a churchgoer). "Or I guess it could be, yes, if faith is the same as fortitude. Your conditioning—you were athletic and in good shape—that's what I think saved you. There is a will to live, and you definitely have that, too." But sometimes the will to live isn't enough. It wasn't for my mother; faith wasn't, either. Travis then said something I'd remember later: "People who want to live fight a lot harder."

WHILE I WAS LYING in the road, before the ambulance came, Joanne, Kevin, and a police officer were with me, all watching for traffic. There really wasn't any. Just one small white car came up the hill. Out jumped the kid who had bagged my groceries the day before. He was new in town. He had red hair. I didn't know his name. I took this to be a terrible omen. After all, my book was titled *If You Lived Here, I'd Know Your Name*. He came close, knelt down next to my head, and asked if he could do anything. His hands shook as he lit a cigarette, inhaled deeply, and exhaled into my face. "Mind if I smoke?" he asked. I almost said, "No, go ahead." That's what I always say, even though I don't like cigarette smoke at all.

But I do like to please. I never want to be confrontational, and I understand smoking is an addiction. Also, we were outside and it's not as if we were eating. He took another puff. The pain radiating out of my back and belly was terrible, the worst you can imagine. It felt like I'd been hit by a truck. It was hard to breathe and I was dizzy. I thought: I don't want my last words to be a lie, especially a lie to make someone like me. I said, "Yes, I do mind if you smoke."

Well, he flicked that cigarette away so far you would have thought it was a lit firecracker. Then he asked if there was anything else he could do for me, and I said to hurry and find my husband. He took off down the hill to our lumberyard, where Chip works. When he was told Chip was at the post office, he raced over there and yelled for him to come quick, which pretty much assured that half the town knew what had happened before I made it to the clinic.

My friend Becky met us there with our daughter J.J. and son, Christian. She had taken them out of school. The youngest, Stoli, was at a track meet in Juneau, the oldest two, Eliza and Sarah, were away at college (remember, I had been painting their rooms). Becky told me later that she thought they would never see me again. The clinic staff cinched my middle together and put me in an air body cast, readying me for the medevac to Seattle. This is how emergencies work in remote Alaskan communities without hospitals. Even the Juneau hospital was too small for this kind of trauma. So they called an air ambulance service that flew a prop ambulance plane up from Juneau and then took Chip and me to Sitka, where I was transferred on a stretcher to an ambulance Learjet that had flown up from Seattle to meet us and bring us the rest of the way. We flew down the coast of Alaska and British Columbia to Seattle's Harborview Medical Center. The jet landed at Boeing Field instead of Sea-Tac Airport because it's closer to the hospital. A four-wheeled ambulance met us there. I don't remember much about what happened that night but know that early the next morning my smashed pelvis was put back together by a team of surgeons, which included, I was told, the best pelvic doctor on the West Coast—maybe in the country—Dr. Chip Routt. I took his name, the same as my husband's, as a good omen.

Six bones were snapped; "teacup fractures" is how the nurse described them. Since the pelvis bones are connected loops, if one side breaks the other does as well, like the handle of a china cup. This is why everything felt squishy. I also cracked my sacrum, that blade in the lower back just above the nub that used to be a tail. Important nerves run through little holes in it. Going into surgery, Dr. Routt's colleague from Texas, Dr. "Please call me Joe" Conflitti, who would operate on me with him, held my hand and said I had a fifty-fifty chance of walking again.

Turns out I got the good half of the odds and, as Becky would say, it was "a miracle" that no organs were harmed.

After a few months in bed, I would learn to walk again. In nine months, the good doctors promised, I'd be 80 percent back to my old self.

When I was able to leave Seattle three weeks later, a wheelchair van took Chip and me to the airport. I was scared when the flight attendants carried me into my seat. I didn't want them to drop me. I was also embarrassed to be wearing a diaper. I wouldn't be able to leave my seat until I was carried off the jet and placed back in my wheelchair in Juneau. It was hard to have to ask for so much help just to enter and exit a plane and to have all those people looking at me, and especially Chip, with such sympathy. My circumstance was temporary. Imagine if this were my life? Our life. Imagine how quickly everything would change if this were your life. Imagine it. What would you do? How would you handle it? This is another reason why Chip kept reminding me that I was very lucky.

I didn't want to wet the diaper, I really didn't. So Chip helped me use the handicapped bathroom in the terminal before boarding the plane. The door to the only unisex one was locked, so we waited for about five minutes. It didn't surprise me. I knew by then that bathroom visits with a wheelchair take a lot longer than they do without one. When the door finally opened, a tailored-suited, blue-tied businessman smelling of cologne strode quickly out. He had left the sink dirty from his shave. I didn't wish he'd get hit by a truck. I wouldn't wish that on anyone.

Instead, I wished Tonya Harding would whack him in the knee really hard with a baseball bat.

As the jet took off, I looked out the window at Seattle dropping away, at the toy houses and ribbon roads with all the little cars moving along them, and at the tiny boats on the flat lakes and wavy sound, and I realized that something was missing. It took being almost killed while doing something so normal, so non-life-threatening as riding a bike down a quiet street in Haines on a sunny April day, to banish my fear of flying. I know it may seem like a small gift, but at the time it was big. With considerable help from OxyContin and morphine, I had been granted what that popular prayer requests: the serenity to accept something I couldn't change. Also, I was so happy to be finally leaving the Sleepless in Seattle Nursing Home that I would have had the courage to take a hang glider home. The extra painkillers they gave me for the long day of traveling made it impossible to concentrate on a book, and there was no movie on the two-and-a-half-hour flight, so I watched one in my head about what "really" had happened that April morning.

It begins with me coasting down the hill overlooking Portage Cove, where skiffs troll in the sunshine for the season's first king salmon. The mountains still have snow on them, and they look so white against the blue, blue sky. The harbor is almost flat calm and a deep blue-green. In the distance a dog barks, a chainsaw starts up, and a small plane banks along the side of Mt. Ripinsky toward

Skagway. I am smiling and happily pedaling through the middle of my life in the middle of an otherwise ordinary morning. I wave to my good friend Joanne, and suddenly a truck pulls out in front of me. Then the scene cuts to God's control room, which is a hybrid of the library at Yale and the CNN set, and that angel Clarence from *It's a Wonderful Life* looks down at me through binoculars and says, "Whoa, Lord, it's not her day yet." He does the best he can to help but, like me, he's a bit of a bumbler. (They can always tell when I'm running up the stairs to the newspaper office, because I usually trip at least once.) So even though he saves me, I still break my pelvis.

This may be part of the reason why, when I saw (in this order) Dave Olerud's son Doug and his dad's wheelchair-accessible van waiting to pick us up at the ferry terminal, the lights of Haines reflecting in Portage Cove on the drive through town, our house, our dogs, our children, and our friend and neighbor Linnus, who had held it all together for us while we were gone, everyone cried but me. Chip was right. I was lucky to be alive and lucky to home. I had been spared to see another day. This day.

Everyone was so proud of the recovery room they'd made me in an alcove of the living room that they wheeled me right over. (We don't have a downstairs bedroom and, remember, my room was now all the way up in the attic.) It seemed as if half the town had helped create my new digs. For the next two months we would be brought dinner every night and more cookies, soups, and casseroles than we could eat. The kids and Linnus had a list of credits for the improvements.

"Nancy got you the hospital bed; it's from the Emblem Club," Christian said. The bed was right in the front window, overlooking the beach, so they had put up a curtain rod and sewed white sheets into drapes for privacy.

"Sue ironed them," J.J. said, then lifted up a heavy shopping bag. "Fan mail. Can you believe it?" It was from readers of my column and the new book.

Stoli showed me the bright quilt Becky had sewed. It was yellow and had chickens on it. "Why did the chicken stay off the road? So it wouldn't get run over by a truck," was written on the corner in fabric marker. Our friend Tim and neighbor Greg made the ramps I'd been wheeled into the house on, and more out the back door so I could sit on the deck in sunny weather. They had built an enclosure on the porch that doubled as an outhouse and shower. (The door of our bathroom wasn't wide enough for my wheelchair.) A hose ran along the outside of the house and through a window so it could be connected to the kitchen faucet for a warm shower. There was a colorful shower curtain and a plastic bench with a potty seat on it.

"That's from the Emblem Club, too," Christian said. He was extra polite and quiet. I wished I could hug him. I regretted fibbing over the phone. I wasn't ever doing wheelies in the nursing home. I had lied when I said Chip and I played cribbage all day and that I beat him. The only time of each day I was peppy was on the phone with the kids. Since I'd been gone, I'd lost about twenty pounds, and my eyes had dark circles around them. I could tell this wasn't what any of them had expected. I would not be able to use the cute back-porch shower and outhouse for weeks. The potty had to be moved inside, closer to my bed. They would all have to learn to slide me on and off it without my feet ever touching the ground. Even though I wasn't paralyzed, it seemed like it since I could bear no weight on my healing bones.

It was after midnight when we said goodbye to Linnus, and I kissed everyone goodnight. Chip tucked me in, and my little dog Phoebe jumped up next to me. The two big dogs thumped their tails at a respectful distance. Chip opened the windows to let the beach air in. The kids had put the screens in for me; they knew I liked the sounds and scents of the beach. In the late spring twilight we call night in Alaska, we listened to the sea lions exhaling, the gulls calling, and the waves meeting the shore. Robert Frost was wrong; there is a greater devotion than the shore to the ocean. It is a husband who will help you with a bedpan and the wiping up, and then say you are beautiful when you look as bad as you ever have in your life. The deep line Chip had been holding in his forehead since the accident softened. There was a lot I wanted to say to him, but all I could manage was "goodnight." He whistled softly as he made up his bed on the window seat at the other end of our living room, where he'd stay until

I got better, so I could call him in the night if I needed to go to the bathroom or to take another pain pill.

"It's really good to be home," he said to the house we had built together, to the beams in the ceiling, to the old Turkish rug from his grandmother's house, to the dogs, to the too many books, to the piano my mother gave us, to our children sleeping upstairs, and beyond the green metal roof and graying shingles to the garden, to the cherry trees and beach roses, to the inlet and Pyramid Island, and to the mountains rising across the way. To grouse in the brush and the bears in the forest and the salmon in the sea, to all of it, he said, "It really is good to be home."

CHAPTER 4

Namaste

You are no longer strangers and sojourners, but
fellow citizens with the saints and members of the
household of God. —Ephesians 2:19

The good news is that a year after my accident I was able to walk, hike, and even run again. Before I could jog, though, I started attending yoga class. At the very end of each class, the instructor, Mandy Ramsey, who has long blonde hair and the sweetest soul you'll ever meet (as well as the most flexible body), puts her hands together as if she is praying, tucks them right next to her heart, and says, "Namaste" (it sounds like nah-mahs-day), and we all respond with the same gesture and word. For weeks after I began the class, I had no idea what it meant but did it anyway, because everyone else did. When in yoga do as the yogis do. This may have been a mistake during the partner part of one class, when a man I didn't know at the time—he's a retired lawyer who recently moved to

Haines—had to hold my legs up on his shoulders while my head stayed on the floor. Instead of giving me a fine stretch, the whole thing felt more like a cross between some sort of weird sex game and the wheelbarrow races on the Fourth of July—the kind in which one person holds the feet of another person who "runs" with her hands across the grass in Tlingit Park. But that was the worst of it. Mostly, doing as the yogis did was all wonderful and left me feeling light in body and soul.

Yoga takes place Tuesday and Thursday evenings in the Chilkat Center dance studio, upstairs in the old cannery building where our Episcopal church also meets. Sometimes, the way we stretch and think in yoga reminds me of church. Jan Hotze, our vicar, doesn't come to yoga, but one Sunday she talked about the term *namaste*, quoting Joan Chittister's book *The Rule of Benedict*. *Vicar* is an old-fashioned Episcopal word that basically means a mission priest who isn't paid. Our congregation provides her a small stipend, but Jan makes her living as a substance abuse counselor for the Haines and Klukwan clinics. She still spends a good deal of time preparing her sermons. Anyway, Jan told us that Chittister writes that *namaste* means the divine in me greets the divine in you, or the Holy Spirit in me touches the Holy Spirit in you. She said that when we encounter people in our life and work, we should be on the alert for holy spirits trying to reveal themselves and that Christians should, as Chittister writes, acknowledge the gifts of God that the other person brings to the meeting, whether they are friend or stranger, arriving or departing.

The other spiritual stretch that happens at the end of every yoga class is that we all lie down on our backs on thick pads with hands crossed on our chests and a warm wool blanket pulled up to our chins. It is called the corpse pose. We rest this way for a few minutes, until three bells ring, then we roll over on our sides, pull our knees up into the birth pose, a fetal position, and wait there a long moment before sitting up, putting our hands together at our hearts, and saying "Namaste" to honor the place of light, love, and truth inside one another, the place Mandy says is where the universe lives in all of us. We die and are reborn twice a week. It's pretty darn symbolic, especially for someone like me who thinks too much about life and death anyway. It does make dying less scary, though, when you practice it for a few moments each week.

I was missing yoga class and thinking about what Jan said in church as I reentered Alaska after a busy week in L.A. with my daughter J.J., then a high school senior, and, as now, a runner. I was missing home, too, although it was great to see J.J. run in a regional cross-country race, take her to the J. Paul Getty Museum, visit some possible colleges, and drive around Hollywood. I also spent a lot of time gripping a steering wheel with all my might and praying we wouldn't die in a terrible crash. It wasn't until I was safely home that the Guy Clarke lyrics, "If I can just get off of this L.A. freeway without getting killed," finally quit running through my head. Technically I wasn't home yet, but I was in Juneau and back on the familiar turf, actually decking, of the northbound ferry for Haines. It was December and so I suppose I shouldn't have been surprised that I would receive the first gift of the season on that boat.

It was dark and cold—five degrees is especially biting in damp Juneau—when J.J. and I lifted our bags onto a luggage cart, one of two open double-decker trailers pulled by a small tractor that resembles a toy train. It was packed with boxes of Christmas presents, duffel bags, suitcases, coolers of groceries, infant car seats—all kept secure by only a vinyl curtain and the honesty of our fellow travelers.

We hustled down the metal boat ramp and onto the brightly lit car deck, where crew members in insulated coveralls exhaled clouds of steam as their mittened hands directed the drivers of cars and trucks to parking spaces. Then we dashed into the heated stairwell, climbed the steep stairs up to the main deck, and headed down the long windowed hall to the cafeteria. Though it was quiet at 6 a.m., familiar faces greeted us from the few occupied tables. The wraparound windows were still black, reflecting what was inside, rather than bringing in the outside views of Auke Bay with its forested shore and rocky islands. The food service line wouldn't open for another hour, but there was hot water and ferry coffee available. My friend Beth was there with a camping

coffee kit—fresh ground beans and a drip cone filter—
and offered to brew me a cup; she even had a thermos of
half-and-half.

Once the strong coffee jump-started us, we fell into a
happy discussion about the birth of her grandson. Beth
and her husband had left Haines back at Halloween and
had taken the ferry all the way to Bellingham and then
driven to San Francisco to be there for the baby's arrival.
The trip cost about the same as flying, she said, but was
so much nicer. What a difference traveling by ship is from
those traffic-filled L.A. freeways. It's why I hope they
never build a road between Haines and Juneau along the
Lynn Canal. It's much more pleasant to eat, drink, walk
around, and visit with friends than worry about traffic,
icy roads, and getting killed in avalanches.

Later, when we arrived home, my weather-watching
neighbor Betty Holgate told me that, according to the
weather service remote control gauges, it was blowing
thirty-five knots from the north with gusts to sixty at El-
dred Rock lighthouse when our ferry went by. But while
on board, we plowed confidently into the steamy gale.
There was some rolling and a few shudders as the heavy
ship surged through the waves, but the cafeteria was
mostly steady. The 408-foot navy blue hulled *Malaspina*
is, as are all the state ferries, named for a glacier. It is more
than forty years old and is one of the original Alaskan ferries that make up what we call the Alaska Marine Highway, a waterway connecting the roadless communities of

southeast Alaska. I like to think of her as our *Queen Mary,* only more democratic. There's no first class; everyone on this boat travels in the same pretty good class.

During breakfast Beth and I chatted, and then kept on chatting about everything big and small, from hens to Jesus. Beth is the kind of vegetarian who eats eggs. I keep chickens. She leans mostly toward the Buddhist philosophy for her inspiration, although she says she thinks of herself as someone who embraces "the tenets of love and compassion that are found in most religions." I'm very Christian, or as Christian as Episcopalians are, which means I go to church and pray and believe but do not, as my more evangelical friends do, preface my opinions with "I'm a Christian . . ." Beth did attend a service at San Francisco's Glide Memorial Church when she was down there and said that if we had a similar church in Haines, she would go more often. Glide's mission is to battle poverty, drug abuse, violence, and prejudice with the unconditional love of Jesus. They also provide job training and help people find employment. That, and they offer lots of free meals and health care. In Haines there isn't any one place that does all that; we all do, often in little and less public displays of charity, like the way my family received all those casseroles when I was hurt, or the way Beth, in her work at Hospice of Haines, makes sure the elderly and ill can stay at home to die. Beth has been and continues to be instrumental in the operation of the local hospice.

• • •

AS SO OFTEN HAPPENS, Beth and I went from being saints to sinners seamlessly, jumping from praising the noble mission of Glide Memorial one minute to criticizing an ornery newcomer to Haines who wrote a belligerent letter to the editor of the *Chilkat Valley News* the next. I said I hoped he would move back to wherever he came from. Beth decided she would shower the combative letter writer's house with thoughts of love and happiness each time she drove or walked by it. Then she lifted her arms and wiggled her fingers like a shaman and laughed.

Beth made more coffee and we talked about colleges. J.J. and I had been looking at schools with good cross-country running programs. Beth had been a marathon runner when she was younger and had attended graduate school at the University of Oregon. Thinking about those days prompted her to talk about a friend of hers, an Olympic sprinter, who had been killed by a sniper. Beth was waiting at a café near campus where they were supposed to meet for lunch when he was gunned down by a crazy man outside the college stadium. A woman from the local hospice had helped Beth make it through those days right afterward. She had found Beth's house, knocked on her door, and then that stranger said she was there to help her grieve.

That's how Beth was introduced to the organization that would become her life's calling. She sipped her coffee and we were both quiet a minute. I was thinking about

J.J. going off to college and snipers, and suddenly I felt so sad. Beth said that her father, a hunter, had told her later that if her sprinter friend had run off in a zigzag pattern instead of a straight line, he probably would not have been shot dead. Then they would still be friends. Then she could send him a card with a photo of the new grandbaby and a cheerful "Time flies!" note. I turned to J.J. and told her to remember the zigzag part if she's ever in a place where someone starts shooting. J.J. rolled her eyes and said, "Oh, Mom, that'll never happen." But it does, and it did, and it will again, I wanted to say. Read the paper, watch TV, listen to the radio. It happens every day, somewhere. Maybe Al should mention this bullet-dodging maneuver in the next Safety Report.

Thinking about so much real and potential loss prompted me to tell Beth about my first hospice client. I wanted to call her *friend* because that is what she became, but at hospice we call the people we read to or help to the bathroom or make lunch for *clients*. Even though Haines is small, we do our best to keep the clients' names, and who is caring for them, confidential. I'm on the hospice board—my editor, Tom, jokes that I became involved so I'd have a heads-up on obituaries—and I had planned to start the volunteer training on the weekend I was run over by the truck. I took it the following spring and was able to use it to help my mother die and my father (I hope) deal with her death. Before all that happened, though, I wasn't sure I was ready to be a hospice volunteer. I do know that following my accident and my mother's death, I was certainly better prepared for the hospice work.

My first hospice client was scheduled to leave town in a couple of days. She was moving into an extended care facility in Anchorage in order to be closer to family there. She had grown up here and had graduated from Haines High, but for the past fifteen years or so had worked for several small Alaskan airlines and as a deckhand on a fishing boat based in a tiny village near Sitka. A hiker and a skier, she had worked in a mostly male industry and was used to pulling crab pots, baiting hooks, and reeling in fish on decks pelted with cold rain in big swells. She was tough and fit. Then a backache turned out to be lung cancer. In early summer she had moved home to Haines to put her affairs in order. By October she was on oxygen and unable to leave her apartment. My instructions were to check in and spend about a half hour a day running errands for her and perhaps make some rice pudding, as she was having trouble keeping food down. Her place was sparse. It looked as though someone was moving out. There were taped boxes against a wall, a few neat stacks of books on the floor, yesterday's newspaper, a lamp, table, and chairs.

The first time I went over, the building's manager was replacing damaged siding. It was raining so hard that he was working under blue vinyl tarps. One blocked my client's window, and she told me that the hammering and the flapping wind and machine-gun rain on the tarp were driving her nuts. (You know, it sounds so formal calling her "my client" or even "my friend" so would it be okay if I call her Marian? That's not her real name, but I think she'd like it, since she loved to read and could sing like the librarian called Marian in *The Music Man,* and using it will not violate the hospice privacy rule.) So, Marian's apartment was dark and noisy. The tarps gave the place a blue hue. It was also hot, and an oxygen machine hummed underneath all that construction clatter and strafing rain. And it was full of cigarette smoke, which I thought was odd. Marian was lying down and reading in a sleeping bag on the floor, pillows propped all around. Her "nest," she called it. The floor felt better on her back than the futon she had been sleeping on.

That day Marian didn't stand up. She handed me written instructions for the grocery store and post office, her mailbox number and key, and the store perks card. She pointed to where everything was: her living will, her insurance papers, her sister's phone number. Marian was organized and completely matter-of-fact about her imminent death, making sure her bills were paid, letters were mailed, and belongings were packed so that when she died her friends and family wouldn't have too much work to do. She even had a suitcase ready with overnight needs in the event of an emergency medevac. Marian was fifty-seven years old and had been told she had five months to live, tops.

Turns out she didn't leave for the Anchorage extended

care facility as she had planned. There were glitches with the admitting paperwork and concerns about taking a commercial flight. I half wished she wouldn't go at all, that maybe she'd just die here. I say "half" because, of course I really didn't want her to die. I'd taken to calling her before I went to bed each night and again while I made my coffee in the morning; then I'd head over to see her a few hours later. Some days she was barely able to talk; others she was up and eating yogurt and smoking a cigarette at the table. One morning Marian asked if I thought she was insane to still be smoking. I didn't tell her that I didn't like smoke or that I had a separate change of clothes just for my visits with her or that each day when I left there I went for a walk, a long walk in the woods, drinking in the fresh air like a cold glass of well water. Instead, I said that I had never been in her position and the last thing I was going to do was judge her. I tried not to cry. Marian laughed, a deep raspy FM-radio-late-night-DJ kind of laugh, and said smoking was stupid and I should damn well say so and not be such a wuss. She was going to quit when her current pack was empty.

We looked at her high school yearbook, and Marian told me all about friends of hers back then, many of whom had stayed in Haines and are now friends of mine. She had spent the first half of her life in Haines, I'd spent my second half, and so we filled each other in on the missing years. In school she had been a singer and an actress. She said she was sorry she missed the Lynn Canal

Community Players' production of *The Music Man* and then sang all about trouble in River City. She had a great voice. She also had an Autoharp and clarinet near her nest-bed, which she apparently played when I wasn't there. Our days together turned into a week, and then the week turned into two. Some days I thought I couldn't be in that smoky apartment another minute, others I wanted to stay all afternoon.

While Marian was preparing for death, I was preparing for winter. I went hunting again for the first time since my accident, high on a cliffy ridge above the Chilkat River. When Chip shot a mountain goat, the gully where it fell was so steep that we couldn't move it without falling further ourselves or risking losing it altogether in another tumble, so we skinned and boned the goat right there. Crampons kept my heels on the sedge-covered slope. The alarming angle made my position more of a lean against a wall than a seat on the ground. The views were breathtaking. I know that's a cliché, but they were—the wide braided Chilkat River valley and the spruce- and hemlock-forested foothills; the brown, red, and golden tundra meadows; the rock and gravel benches; and finally the glacial peaks that made up the mountains all around us. We were so high up and it was so steep that if I'd turned around to grab the plastic sheet I'd packed to clean the goat on, I would have slipped and fallen. I had to debone the heavy hindquarters right on my lap, and blood leaked all over my jacket and pants. I couldn't help but think about the other time when I'd had blood on my jacket and pants. I thought about my own bones and flesh as I touched the goat's pelvis and hip bones. The muscle and nerves and sinews that had held him together were so much like mine. I thought about all of that, but not for too long, since there was a lot of work to do. I have done this enough now that I am skilled at it, but I remain surprised that I can cut warm flesh off bone. I'm not sure how or when it happened that I became steady enough to traverse steep ridges and skin just-killed animals. In some ways, it's not much different from the kind of courage it takes to change a stranger's bedpan or help a dying person bathe. It can be done, it really can, by ordinary people. It takes courage is all.

A few days later my body was still sore from the effort of the climb and the pack, and my heart hurt, too, because my friend Marian was becoming worse. She slept more and talked less. She needed more painkillers. She made fewer lists. She told me the only painting on her wall, a watercolor, should go to her sister. One morning we talked about what she wanted in her obituary, and she showed me the photo she had chosen to run with it. It looked like her, only with hair and sparkle. I had known Marian only when she was bald and frail. She had been a stunningly attractive woman. She also told me that she wanted a memorial plaque down in Pelican, the village where she had lived and fished. The tiny boardwalk community on a rocky outcrop doesn't have a cemetery, but it does have a gazebo with bronze burial plaques. Each holds up to three lines, with ten characters each. Thinking about what to put in the lines reminded me of writing a haiku. It was harder than you'd think. Marian took a break and lit a cigarette. She hadn't quit when the last pack ran out. She was smoking more, and there was a carton of menthol lights on my new grocery list. Again she said, "You probably think I'm crazy not to quit."

I said she was the bravest person I had ever known.

MARIAN LISTENED TO the radio but didn't have a computer or a TV and couldn't make it to the library to read the news she craved online. Part of my caregiving was to buy her the daily papers from Anchorage and Juneau. In the summer you can sometimes get the Tuesday papers on Tuesday, but in stormy October and November we are lucky to have them flown into Haines at all. One Thursday, while we were reading the Sunday papers in her now-quiet apartment—the construction was finished, the rain had turned to snow, and the blinds were closed to keep the bright whiteness out—we talked about a whole section devoted to the release of *Into the Wild*, the movie set in Alaska and directed by Sean Penn. Neither of us had seen the film (we don't have a theater here, so I had to wait for the DVD to watch it; Marian didn't live that long), but we both had read Jon Krakauer's book of the same name, about Chris McCandless wasting away and dying in that bus out in the bushes, and we were curious about the reviews. Many of our fellow Alaskans' responses to the film were scathing and cruel and not so much directed at the movie itself, but rather the subject, its boy hero. But I felt differently.

I agree with every Alaskan I know, and I bet every one you do, too, that Chris McCandless was foolishly unprepared. It bothers me that Marian will have a small plaque, and he has a book and now a movie that apparently treats him like a latter-day Thoreau. Chris McCandless walked into the Alaskan wilderness, planning on spending months alone, with just ten pounds of rice and a .22. A hundred years ago a typical Klondike gold seeker brought two hundred pounds of rice and a bigger gun. In Haines and nearby Skagway, fourteen miles up Taiya Inlet from here and where most of the miners began their hikes into the Canadian Yukon Territory, and on up to Bonanza Creek and Dawson City, even grade-schoolers know the Mounties wouldn't let anyone into the backcountry who didn't have a ton of supplies—a full year's provisions—including four hundred pounds of flour, dried fruit, tools, sleds, cookware, and cabin-sized wall tents with woodstoves. Some even hauled materials to build boats.

The *Into the Wild* critics up here, though, don't seem to acknowledge that everyone may not be able to be quite that prepared. I have five children, so I am also well aware that you can't always convince kids to take care of themselves, and I know from reading the book that the young man was troubled. Maybe what really bothers me most

about the barbed comments is the declaimers' inability to
see that Chris McCandless was a real person, a genuine
lost soul. Sure, we may think he made mistakes, but calling him an idiot for being so naive is a little like calling
Marian stupid for smoking. There's truth and then there's
the whole truth. There is now a bronze memorial plaque
in that abandoned junker bus where he died, too, on that
washed-out road thirty miles from anywhere. It memo-
rializes him as a beloved son. When his parents hiked
in, or maybe four-wheeled or snow-mobiled in, to see for
themselves where their boy had died of starvation, they
brought the plaque with them and installed it there in his
memory. His mother left something else behind, too: a
small suitcase of survival gear so this would not happen
to another woman's son who for whatever reason may call
that bus home or stumble on it during a wilderness trek.
She put a first-aid kit, map, blankets, and a can of tuna
fish in the suitcase. To the first person who needs it, that
suitcase will be like a gift from God; the divine in her will
meet the divine in a stranger. Namaste.

When we were struggling to figure out what to say on
Marian's plaque, the three lines that the world would remember her best by, she quoted Woody Allen, joking that
she didn't want to live in my or anyone else's memory;
she'd prefer her own apartment.

I THOUGHT ABOUT THAT, and how glad I was
to be returning home and how important my own well-

stocked house is to me, while Beth and I sat in the dining room of that northbound ferry talking about life and death and especially Marian. I said that I wished more than anything in the world that she hadn't smoked, that she hadn't had lung cancer, that she hadn't died. I told Beth that Marian and I had talked about death in the way I had hoped my mother and I could have but never did. I told her how I had thought I was volunteering to help a dying person but that in lots of ways she had helped me more than I helped her because she was so frank, so willing to let me help, so close to whatever there is on the other side of this life. Marian had the kind of spirit that was a comfort to glimpse, even as it was leaving her. Beth said I was lucky. Just like Chip said I was lucky in that wheelchair. You know, sometimes, I wish I weren't quite so lucky.

We were still talking, quietly and more seriously now, when we realized the cafeteria was empty. The ferry had docked in Haines and my (thank goodness) very healthy friend Joanne, who works out at the ferry terminal, selling tickets and securing ships to the big old pilings, the same friend who had helped make sure I didn't die that day in the road next to her house, was down on the dock in her life vest, tying up our boat. Beth embraced me as we parted. She didn't say "Namaste," but she might as well have.

MARIAN WROTE HER OWN obituary. In the end, I couldn't even do that for her. She was a good writer. The details were sharp. She wrote that she was "a precocious child who learned to read at the age of three." Writing of herself in the third person, she noted, "Despite her discomfort during her illness, she continued to manifest her sense of humor, asking the staff at Providence [an Anchorage hospital], 'Okay, anyone who's surprised I have lung cancer after smoking three packs a day for forty-five years, raise your hands. Don't be shy. Get those hands up where I can see them!'" In lieu of flowers, she requested donations be made to Hospice of Haines.

After the drive from the ferry to our house, I unpacked and cooked my family a nice dinner, setting the table with candles and my mother's china and silver. I was grateful to have so much. Later, when Chip had done all the dishes and gone upstairs to read and the woodstove was loaded and damped down for the night, I let the dogs out one last time. I like being outside at night. I like hearing the waves meet the shore and the wind in the trees. I like looking at the stars. I sat on the steps in my old wool duffle coat, ski hat, and the mittens Eliza knitted me last Christmas and found the Pleiades and Orion's belt. I am fascinated by the night sky, which I suppose is a good thing, since for much of the year Alaska has more of it than anywhere else in the United States. When it's clear, I check on the heavens before I go to bed. I have also bought an astronomy guidebook and am learning about the constellations. So I stared up at all the twinkling lights and celestial smudges for a long time. When I saw a shooting star, I made a wish that my children will outlive me. I waited for another star to zip bottle-rocket-style across the sky. When one did, I wished that Marian was in heaven. I thought about my mother and about Beth's college sprinter who had been shot and about my accident and about Chris McCandless's mother and that survival suitcase. I was getting cold, but still I waited for one more shooting star. When it appeared, I wished for another ordinary day, one just like today, where the divine in me greets the divine in so many others, both here and gone and somehow all mixed up in holy spirits. Namaste.

CHAPTER 5

Take Good Care of the Garden and the Dogs

Father of mercies and giver of all comfort:
Deal graciously, we pray thee, with all who mourn.
—Book of Common Prayer

It is more than a little strange that while the only thing we know for sure about life is that we will die, each time it happens most of us are surprised. Not just by the instant, shocking deaths—a plane crash or a heart attack between salad and dessert—but even the ones caused by illnesses that we know are terminal.

Our family knew, more or less, that my mother was not going to live past seventy. She was fifty-four when she was diagnosed with chronic lymphocytic leukemia and given about fifteen years to live, barring any other calamity and so long as she followed the recommended course of treatment. That meant regular blood tests and chemotherapy when the results showed her rogue white blood cells were taking over. CLL, as it is called by us unlucky folks in the know, is a cancer of the white blood cells (lymphocytes) and, in particular, the B cells, which normally fight infection. With CLL, the DNA of the B cell is damaged and thus can't fight contagion. Some people live a long time with CLL, up to twenty-five years. It depends on how far advanced it is when discovered, how aggressive it is (some people have it and never need treatment), how strong you are, and how old you are, since it usually occurs in people over fifty. If you develop CLL when you are eighty, you probably won't have another quarter century. That said, somehow it still came as a shock when a few months after my mother's seventy-first birthday she became very sick.

The real surprise, though, was that she didn't say, "I'm ready to die. I've had a good life, let's skip the medical gymnastics and call it a day." In mid-February we learned that her course of chemotherapy, which had left her hairless and weak, was not working. My own recovery *had* been working, and the only good thing about the timing of my mother's illness was that I was strong enough, my broken pelvis sufficiently on the mend, for me to travel from Alaska to New York to be with her.

Way back when my mother was about the same age I am now, she had chosen to manage, rather than attempt to cure, her type of leukemia. When you are in your fifties, seventy can seem like forever. We all kind of forgot about her deadline, partly because she seemed so healthy and partly because she never mentioned it. There were monthly blood draws and, when results warranted, she would be given a mild oral chemotherapy to ensure white and red cells were at the levels they needed to be. She remained so fit that while I was in the hospital after my accident, she was, too, except she was recovering from a hip replacement she had elected to go through in order to play golf without pain. She won another club championship that summer. Ten months later she was fighting, I mean really fighting, for her life.

I never worked up the courage to speak to my mother about choosing hospice care, even though I'm now a hospice volunteer. I never told her about the hospice philosophy, which is linked to the belief that death is a natural part of life, that it can be managed so people can remain alert and as pain free as possible until the end, and that death is as much a spiritual and emotional experience as it is a physical one, for all involved. If I had said that, though, I'm pretty sure my mother would have replied, "You must be joking." And that's okay. It was her life and it would be her death, and the very least I could do was not make her do it my way. I mean, if dying isn't an excuse to put your own wishes first, what is?

WHENEVER I TALKED to Mom on the phone she'd say she was "a little anemic." When my dad called after she was asleep, he'd tell me that she was really sick and that nothing was making her better. I asked him if I should come home. "Could you?" he asked. "That would be great." I love my father and he had rarely requested much, so I booked a flight to New York and a week later moved into the guest room of my parents' Dutchess County farmhouse.

Right away we decided that my sister Kathleen, who lives with her family on the same farm as my parents, and I would find out how much time my mother had to live. We would ask the doctor what "the prognosis" was, as my father kept calling it. Dad had tried to find out himself, but his inquiries to doctors about white blood cells, hemoglobin, and types of treatment drove my mother batty, especially the way he wrote everything down in his pocket diary and reread the notes at the breakfast table each morning, hypothesizing on their meaning. He knew everything except what really mattered.

Kathleen and I would take my mother to her next appointment and speak with the doctor privately. We cleared this arrangement with my mother, who agreed. The doctor's clinic was in a pretty, antique white house on a leafy street in nearby Sharon, Connecticut. The plan was for Kathleen and me to ask him a few questions about my mother—Was she dying? Would she get well? What can we expect? Was it hospice time?—while she sat in the waiting room, which looked more like a prep school admissions office than a health clinic, reading Joan Didion's *The Year of Magical Thinking*. My sister had bought it for her as a Christmas gift but changed her mind after the downturn in her health. My mother had spied the book on Kathleen's kitchen counter and said she wanted to read it. When Kathleen suggested that it might not be the best book right now—it is, after all, about the sudden death of Didion's husband, followed by the death of her only daughter—my mother replied, "Kathleen, I am not dying and no one in our family is."

As I said, the plan was for a private discussion with the doctor, but my mother decided to come into the office with us. The doctor held my mother's hand and told us how courageous she was. My sister and I looked at those overlapped hands with wonder. We already knew that my mother was strong and brave. This softness was a surprise. We had never held my mother's hands like that; she never held ours that way, either. I was a little jealous, and I could tell Kathleen was, too. We made "What the hell?" eye contact. Then the doctor told us, while looking earnestly at our mother, that the treatments hadn't worked. However, he had faith in an experimental new biological therapy. I think it was something about replacing the damaged B cells with healthy ones. My sister, along with my father, was becoming an expert in all of this, thanks to *The Merck Manual*. I remained, perhaps willfully, confused by medical terminology. I am apparently my mother's daughter, as I'd rather not know. The doctor wanted to start the next day. He would deliver the treatment intravenously from one of the comfortable recliners in what was really the living room of his clinic-house. It was all very un-institutional. My mother, who it turned out was also a bit of a magical thinker, would finish that book there. Joan Didion is an Episcopalian, as was my mother, who must have appreciated the references to the Cathedral Church of St. John the Divine in Manhattan. She must have nodded her head with understanding when Didion quoted from the burial service in the Book of Common Prayer: "In the midst of life we are in death." She must have, although she never said so. Her doctor never did answer our unspoken questions, either. He didn't blurt out, "If this works your mother will have six more months" or "If this doesn't work, she's looking at two to four months" or even "If this works she'll have to replace that other hip." He did ask my mother if she had any questions. She said no.

For the next several days I took my mother to her treatments. Then we rested and waited a week until another round of tests would determine if they had worked. One afternoon, while she was lying on the sofa by the fire, a country neighbor came by, an elderly woman I didn't know and with whom my mother had only recently become acquainted. She brought a blue and white cachepot for my mother's flowers. Mom was a great gardener and, when I was young, kept a greenhouse full of orchids in our backyard on Long Island. That afternoon, blue hydrangeas, hyacinths, and red geraniums bloomed on the library table abutting the sofa. Sun streamed in the tall windows of the barn-like room. The spry, gray-haired gal—she was in her eighties—gave my mother the pot, announcing almost cheerfully that she had just been told she had only months to live and was giving away all her possessions to people now, rather than wait for her family to do so after she died. She knew my mother liked flowers and thought she could use the pretty container. After she left—in a hurry because she apparently had a car full of treasures to distribute—my mother laughed and said that if she were ever dying she'd like to do the same thing.

MY MOTHER HAD ALWAYS been a walker, taking long, hard treks for an hour or two daily. All three of her daughters also favor the brisk walks that the men in our family jokingly compare to the Bataan Death March. One afternoon I realized that they had it wrong. Those long walks weren't death marches. It was my mom's new, short, slow ones that were, and there wasn't anything funny about them. Mom and I were walking carefully back from her mailbox over the hillcrest of the dirt road between a hay field and a herd of Black Angus cattle when Reggie pulled up next to us. Reggie works on my parents' farm and on other farms in the neighborhood. As soon as I arrived and my father was off full-time caregiver duty, he and Reggie had begun cleaning the underbrush and downed trees from a stand of pines by the road. Reggie, who is in his eighties, cut the dead wood, and my dad, who is in his early seventies, hauled it to the burn pile.

Reggie keeps nitroglycerin tablets handy because he has "a bad ticker." He uses *goddamn* not as a swear word, but for added emphasis. His wife's cooking is goddamn good, politicians are goddamn bad, and the goddamn tractor he wants to sell my dad is a goddamn nice machine. Reggie pulled up beside Mom and me and rolled down the window of his pickup, observing that it was a goddamn fine day, which it was. The weather was unseasonably mild, and the rolling hills of the Catskills' brown fields and gray winter forests repeated as far as we could see. A jet drew white lines in the pale blue sky, way up high, so high we couldn't hear it. Reggie looked at my mother's colorless skin, the fleece hat covering her bald head, the loose clothing, and asked, "Do you like molasses?" My mother frowned a "no," dismissing him. She had been a high school principal after all. And she was not in the mood for Reggie, who tipped his cap and drove off down the muddy driveway, one hand on the wheel, the other quickly rolling up the window.

The next afternoon Mom and I were reading outside on the patio by her still-dormant garden, in the continuing warm sunshine. Out of the wind as we were, it must have been sixty degrees, but Mom wore a down coat and had a wool blanket on her lap. We were both sitting in teak deck chairs. Her Labradors slept in the sun on the blue stone. I had brought her some tea and told her to pretend we were on a trans-Atlantic cruise. My mother snorted that I always did have a good imagination.

Dad and Reggie were down in the lower field. My father saw us and hiked over the brown stubble to share a story he said Reggie wanted him to tell Mom. (I suppose

Reggie was still a little shy of my mother after the encounter the day before.) Reggie told Dad that when he was a kid there was a bachelor sanitation man who hauled away septic tank sludge in barrels using a horse-drawn wagon. It was hard, dirty work but he did it with a smile. The sanitation man lived with his mother and was devastated when she was told she had stomach cancer. He moped around so badly people worried he might die with her, of a broken heart. The poor old woman clearly did not have long to live.

I was thinking that this was not such a good story to tell. I made eye contact with my dad, hinting that he should change the subject, but Dad plowed on. The woman, seeing her son's concern, told him to bring her a pail of molasses. She sipped the whole thing up with a straw and, as Reggie told my father who told my mother, it turned out that she drank a gallon of molasses every day for a year. Now Dad raised his voice and clapped his hands and said with a chuckle, "Sal, the goddamn molasses killed the goddamn cancer." My mother usually went by the name Sally but my father called her Sal or sometimes Sweet Sarah, since Sarah was her real name. This is a family custom: I am often Heath, or Baby Heather — why I don't know — and Kathleen is Kath, or sometimes Kath-a-leen, and our younger sister Suzanne is Sweet Sue or Two-dan. My father is Papa Bob to his grandchildren, Dad to me, and calls himself Macho Man, The Legend, or even Bobbie V. Our high school boyfriends, who lived in fear of him, dubbed him The Bobber. But you don't need to know all that to appreciate that when my father asked my mother if she liked molasses, she didn't say no and she didn't get mad. She laughed.

MY FRIEND AND HAINES neighbor Madeleine also had chronic lymphocytic leukemia. Diagnosed when she was fifty-nine, she died at sixty-one. She didn't drink gallons of molasses, but for nearly a year she did consume about twenty pounds of vegetables and fruits a day, in juice form. She drank a glass of carrot or green veggie juice every hour, as part of the Gerson method of alternative cancer therapy. Her husband, Fred, and their grown children, Darren and Melina, and her friends volunteered to make the juice, plus share the task of cleaning the juicer and the muslin filters. Though Fred, who went on the program, too, lost weight and said he felt much healthier, it didn't cure Madeleine's CLL or make her feel all that great. Always thin, she grew even more so. It was also extremely time-consuming, so she switched to a macrobiotic diet, eating only whole grains, vegetables, and miso soup. That made her feel better. Finally she decided to combine both diets with the organic food that she had always eaten, and that made her feel the best she had in months. Unlike my mother, she never opted for chemotherapy or any conventional treatment.

Christmas Day at our house is a big, noisy, potluck kind of affair, and the Christmas before she died Madeleine came early, stayed late, and ate everything, even

Sue's green bean casserole—you know the kind, made with cream of mushroom soup and canned fried onions. She said she hadn't felt that good in a long time. She had stopped worrying about her blood tests results, since there was nothing she could do about them. Actually, I don't think she ever did have the type of regular tests my mother had. Madeleine was an artist and didn't have health insurance, partly because of the cost but mainly because she didn't really believe in Western medicine.

On New Year's Eve, Madeleine and Melina snowshoed on Mt. Ripinsky and then Madeleine went to her friends Gershon and Kerry's house. The Cohens live in the woods, about five miles out of town. Their home is above their pottery studio. The trio spent the evening lighting candles for people dear to their hearts. They brought clay up from the studio to the dining table and rolled balls to create candle bases. They placed about seventy small Chanukah candles and a dozen larger candles that they also had in the house all around the room—on the windowsills, the table, the floor, the stereo, the chairs. Then they took turns lighting a candle and naming someone they loved. Madeleine lit the first candle for Melina. Her second candle was for Darren. She lit one for her friend Kerry, and Kerry lit for one for her. Then Madeleine lit one of the large candles for her husband. Fred was in Florida that week. She and Kerry continued until every candle was lit. Then they sat listening to soft, sweet clarinet music in the glow of all of that flickering love.

After Fred returned, he and Madeleine were taking

advantage of the long Alaskan winter nights and falling snow to talk about issues of the heart and home when Madeleine was struck with fierce stomach pains. They thought it was appendicitis, and she was flown to the hospital in Anchorage, where doctors established that it was the end stages of CLL. The white cells had swollen her organs and taken over her digestive system. There was talk of chemotherapy, but she was too weak. She died two extraordinary days later.

I LEFT MY PARENTS' house in mid-February but my mother's condition worsened. My youngest sister, Suzanne, flew in to help her through a splenectomy. When she needed to return to her younger family, I arrived to help my mother die, or so I thought. But Mom was not interested in dying. In fact, she worked as hard as she could at staying alive. There were tests, surgery, medications, a ventilator—everything doctors and hospitals could do, and all with my mother's blessing. As Travis Reid had said about my own survival, she, too, had the kind of will to live that made her fight death a lot harder than some people would have. I was still not completely recovered from my injuries, and before we drove in to Mt. Sinai Hospital in Manhattan each day to see Mom, I spent the early morning hours furtively trotting, testing my limbs and spirit. My treatment had involved a regimen of physical therapy, acupuncture, massage therapy, swimming, and walking. I looked okay, but I had to think about where to place my still-numb right foot with each step. Despite arthritis, my dad also works out every day. All through my mother's hospitalization, he never broke his routine. Maybe Dad's hobbled gait and dogged determination gave me the nerve to try out my running legs. Still, on those mornings, we went our separate ways, both glad for the time outside and that no one was with us to witness the struggle we were having emotionally with Mom's leaving and physically with our own aging and broken bodies. But the day after my mother died, we wanted to be together; we didn't want to run or walk alone. It was raining and cool that morning. "This would be a good day in Alaska," Dad said, adjusting his baseball cap before we stepped off the porch into the drizzle. We talked about a lot of things, big and small, including the funeral, which would be in a hundred-year-old Episcopal church, and what readings and hymns to choose. My father said we had to have the one about "in my house are many mansions," and the Twenty-third Psalm, and he wanted to sing "The strife is o'er, the battle done / The victory of life is won" because it fit my mother well.

Spring in the Hudson Valley is a gift. Daffodils spill down hillsides in front of old farmhouses and show up in odd places. One yellow bouquet appeared at the base of a lonely telephone pole between two dairy farms, just when I needed them most. Who, I wondered, planted those bulbs, and did she or he know what comfort they'd bring to a stranger years hence? In my garden I have transplanted daylilies from my mother's yard and dwarf blue columbine that originated in Madeleine's garden. I also have big orange Asiatic lilies, which grow in just about every garden in Haines. They supposedly came here with Chinese cannery workers in the nineteenth century. Sometimes you see them in the bushes by the beach, marking old cabin sites; sometimes they are all that remain of a garden, or a gardener. I like how hardy they are, and how cheerful and eternal.

In New York, I had been spending sleepless nights unable to shake the images of my mother in her last days. She was supposed to die a weathered old gal on the golf course, digging in her garden, or even dozing by the fire after dinner, in a Shetland sweater with a book on her chest. Not all pale and blotchy and hairless in an ugly old hospital gown, with daffodils in a jar on her windowsill. They were meant to brighten up her room, but they looked too out of place surrounded by all that plastic and metal. In the ten days since we had taken my mother off life support, she had tenaciously hung on to life. She never really regained consciousness. She never really spoke. And there was that one eyebrow I told you about, the one that was perpetually raised in a question mark, which gave her a worried look, but that was all. My mother was a lifelong churchgoer, a devout Episcopalian; she believed in Jesus and heaven, all of it. She went to Bible study class and sang in the choir. All I can think of is that maybe there was one thing she had wanted to tell us before she left—and that's why she had refused to let go. Had she been waiting for something? My mother's heart wouldn't quit even though everything else had. I thought of the line in the Easter Gospel reading, when Jesus asks Peter to stay up with him all night, and Peter promises to, but keeps falling asleep, and Jesus says, "The heart is willing, but the flesh is weak."

Running with my dad a few days after my mom died, I asked him if we should add cream to our coffee instead of skim milk or maybe work out a little less because a quick heart attack would be so much kinder than what she went through. "God, no," he said, as we raced to the mailbox—he always sprints at the end. "This isn't about living longer. It's about the quality of life. Besides, it's keeping us both sane."

"Maybe," I huffed, and he picked up the pace even more while going off on a crazy riff about hospitals, doctors, and the creepy palliative care nurse who looked like Morticia Addams. We had to stop because we were laughing so hard that we were crying, or maybe it was the other way around.

After we caught our breath, Dad pointed through the fog toward a pond across the field. A couple of clumps of daffodils bloomed bright yellow. "Your mother made me go down there with her and plant those on a miserable cold day last fall. I said they'd never grow and that it was too late to plant them. We had a big argument about it. But you know your mother. She didn't take no for an answer." We stood there in the wet morning, steaming from the run, quiet for a few minutes. Then my dad took off his cap and wiped sweat or rain or something else from his eyes and said, "It's not like in the movies, is it?"

No it wasn't, which is why I had figured that scenes and stories of enlightening deathbed gatherings were fiction until Madeleine died.

Her family really did gather around her hospital bed in the hours before. She was awake and lucid and looked, Melina said, "incredibly beautiful." Melina asked if there was anything she wanted to be sure her friends in Haines knew, any last words, and Madeleine said, "The usual, just tell them I love them and everything." To her family, she said, "No guilt." When Darren promised to plant something in her memory, she said that would be very nice and, ever the practical gardener, added, "But if it dies, don't worry about it." She was relaxed, funny even—and not just from the morphine but from an inner kind of strength and wisdom that we all knew she had. She spoke to Darren and Melina and made sure it was okay for her to leave them. At one point a nurse came in with a meal tray and, when Madeleine asked what she was doing, a doctor replied, "She apparently thinks you should be dining instead of dying," and Madeleine said, "Don't they know what we're trying to do here?"

MADELEINE'S MUCH-PHOTOGRAPHED flower, fruit, and vegetable garden overlooking the Port Chilkoot dock was in her front yard. There were pink foxgloves, blue delphiniums, mounds of lavender (which is hard to grow in this climate), raspberries, strawberries, poppies, and Sitka roses. She grew garlic and brussels sprouts, greens and carrots, peas and beans. Her lawn was shaded by sweet cherry and heirloom apple trees. Pots of brightly colored annuals decorated her porch. There was even a white picket fence and winding brick path. It was, in many ways, Haines's front yard. It was — and I should say still is, as her family tends it today — one of the first places cruise ship passengers visited and where neighbors gathered on summer afternoons. Since 1981 she and Fred and later the children have lived, worked, and gardened on Soap Suds Alley in their historic home, first as renters, then as owners, turning the house, their Wild Iris art shop, and especially the place known as "Madeleine's Garden," into a natural and artistic haven. Madeleine was talented, but she was truly humble about her accomplishments, especially her great green thumb. A committed composter, she gave the dirt all the credit.

Just about everything in Madeleine's home and garden was beautiful and useful. Her tidy art studio was adjacent to her kitchen. In it she made cards, T-shirts, paintings, prints, drawings, and jewelry that were sold in the shop on the other side of her living room. Her garden was a kind of painting, too. Well before Madeleine even became ill, she donated a print to Hospice of Haines for a fundraiser. It was of a pastel that she had drawn of the garden and which HOH had printed on coffee mugs.

For Madeleine's service, the Chilkat Center theater was

overflowing, and the stage was full of flowers. Frankie
Jones and her mother, Linda, and sister Jessie shipped
them up from Seattle and arranged them to look like Madeleine's garden. When someone dies in Haines, donations
to a local cause are usually given "in lieu of flowers," but
you couldn't separate Madeleine from flowers in life or
in death. The women's choir, of which both Melina and
I are members, all wore Madeleine's sparkling necklaces
as we sang "Dona Nobis Pacem" ("Grant Us Peace") and
an Irish tune using Emily Dickinson's poem about hope
being the thing with feathers that perches in the soul as
lyrics. I gave the eulogy, a first for me. Laurie, the acu-
puncturist, read a Mary Oliver poem and asked everyone
to be quiet for a very long moment of silence, although she
told parents it was okay to let little children play or talk
or cry because "it's their nature." Afterward Chip said the
sounds the babies made in that stillness reminded him of
the way birds sound in a garden. "They were chirping,"
he said. "I really liked that part."

Pizza Joe read a poem he had composed in Madeleine's
honor, noting that even the bugs left Madeleine's garden
alone, and that God had a new gardener now. There was
a slide show, during which Debra played the piano. The
service ended with Nancy Nash (her husband and Becky's
are related) and her daughter Amelia performing that
Beatles song that goes, "In my life, I've loved you more,"
a beautiful tune about all the people we love in our lives,
and how "some are dead and some are living." I heard it

with new ears and thought how wise those four boys from Liverpool were when they wrote and recorded that.

Writing Madeleine's obituary I learned that after graduating from the University of Illinois with a BA in art, she worked for WGN-TV in Chicago as a set designer, and that our Madeleine, who never watched television, actually designed the set of the original *Phil Donahue Show*. I also learned that she was walking down LaSalle Street one day when a man jumped to his death from a building, landing literally right behind her. (See, this is why I told J.J. that anything that you imagine can happen, might.) Shortly after that, in August 1974, her purse was snatched and she chased the thieves and got it back. Well, it was no wonder that she took both those events as signs that she should leave Chicago, and soon. She and Fred were dating at the time, and he came to the same conclusion. Three years and 180,000 miles later they had car-camped and hiked in all of the lower forty-eight states, driving in Fred's 1972 Capri. Alaska was the forty-ninth state and the final stop—Madeleine loved Haines and they stayed. They had paused long enough in Louisville, Kentucky, to be married by a minister in a cemetery chapel. Madeleine, always a good dresser, wore a form-fitting, short blue dress. Flamboyant Fred had on a textured tie and a wild plaid sport coat.

Madeleine taught her children what she knew but praised them even when they didn't exactly model her own style. Of Melina's paintings, she often said, with pride, that they were "way out there." At her deathbed, Melina read Madeleine a note from her friend Linda, the same Linda who arranged the flowers for her service and who also helped care for Madeleine during her weak, juicing-diet days. In the note, Linda wrote that Jesus was waiting in heaven for Madeleine with His arms wide open. Madeleine replied, "Yes, I know, and all of the other ones [are, too]."

Her ashes were at her service, in a wooden urn turned and carved by friends. Some would be scattered on Mt. Ripinsky, some in her garden, and some might stay on the shelf in her home. Her family and friends aren't ready to part with all of Madeleine just yet.

MY FATHER KEPT my mother's ashes for a while, too, scattering some in her rose bushes and planting some by a paper birch tree, before burying the rest that fall in the family plot at the Woodlawn Cemetery in the Bronx. In the urn with the ashes, he also put sheet music for the piano, the program from her funeral back in April, a golf tee and a ball marker, the name tags of all her beloved Labs, and his finisher's medal from the New York City Marathon.

I believe, as Thornton Wilder wrote in *Our Town,* that there is surely something eternal about every human being. I even believe in heaven. But sometimes that isn't enough, which may explain the folded and well-creased $8\frac{1}{2} \times 11$ piece of paper wedged into my wallet with the heading "Treatment Day Snacks." It's a form listing food and drinks suitable for counteracting or avoiding the side effects of chemotherapy. On the back, in my mother's oh-so-familiar handwriting, are her last grocery lists. She used up the whole page, folding and refolding with each shopping reminder. One fold reveals apricots, cukes, small garbage bags, pie for dessert. My mother wasn't a baker but she enjoyed something sweet after dinner.

Another fold lists leeks, lettuce, bread. Turn it over and there's a new list. Were green tea, Comet cleanser, and grapefruits in her basket on her final trip to the store, or were baking potatoes, O.J., and coffee? I have kept my mother's shopping list because I cannot bear not to, and because it reminds me how quickly we go from here to gone. Also, there is something so brave about keeping the kitchen stocked when you are dying. I found the paper in the pocket of her raincoat, the knee-length model I usually don't wear. I favor rain jackets and pants with rubber boots, the kind of rain gear made for southeast Alaska, where Madeleine once gardened and walked to the grocery store in the windy wet, and where I continue to. But when we were cleaning out my mother's closet after her funeral, my father asked me to take it, so I did.

Lately I have been thinking a lot about the way my mother died and the way Madeleine died. I had been a little angry that my mother never mentioned death before she fell into a coma. That she didn't say goodbye or speak final wise words. She didn't even go out holding our hands. She died in her sleep, all alone, right after we had left the hospital to have lunch.

But before her last surgery, which she requested in order to find out what was causing her lungs to fill with fluid, my dad sat next to her gurney in the preoperating room. He asked her if there was anything she wanted him to know, anything at all she wanted to be sure her friends and family knew, just in case. She was intubated and couldn't speak. She didn't say, as Madeleine had, that she loved us. Instead, she wrote, in the same handwriting as the grocery list I keep refolding, "Take good care of the garden and the dogs!" (The exclamation point is hers.) It was the last coherent communication we had with her.

I HAVE BEEN PUTTING my garden to bed for the winter. It is a long way from my mother's upstate New York farm, but out here in the yard I feel close to her. We had gardening in common. I missed the small burial service for her urn because I was at the state cross-country running championships with the team that I coach. This year the team includes two of my daughters, J.J. and Stoli. They are, in some startling ways, much like my mother. J.J. is so cool under pressure, unflappable, and Stoli is musical—she plays the piano like my mother did and, sometimes, when she can't work out the fingering to a new piece, says, "Oh nuts," just like she heard my mother say. She has been playing one of my mother's favorite Beethoven sonatas and I can hear it now, through the open window. This change of seasons means I light the woodstove to take the chill out each morning, but by mid-day the house is hot enough to open a window or two.

I look up at the clouds and tell Mom about the cross-country race and how well her granddaughters ran. I tell her some other news, too, as I bring in the geraniums from the window boxes and push the wheelbarrow down the path to the beach to gather seaweed for mulch. Tearing down the dead pea vines is satisfying work. But pulling up a handful of the last sweet carrots is like saying goodbye to someone I love. I don't look in the empty holes. I can't do it without thinking of all the people who once filled up my life and now have left it a little emptier. As the song goes, I've loved them all. I look out at the beach. The tide is ebbing, a gull bounces in the turbulence before making a landing on a log, and I wonder again what my mother would have said, had she been able, or willing, to share her last thoughts with us. The more I think about it, the more I start to realize that my mom's final grocery list contains plenty of wisdom about how to live the second half of my life without her.

Maybe it is wishful thinking, or maybe I didn't have enough for lunch and am light-headed, but what I hear her notes, and thus her, imparting, is this: eat dessert, be sure there's coffee for the morning, write things down so you won't forget them, and don't waste paper. And I remember what she told my dad, when he asked if there was anything at all she wanted us to know. "Take good care of the garden and the dogs!" I put some more mulch on my strawberry patch and then I throw a stick for my own dogs, relieved that I haven't missed something big after all, knowing that a person could do worse than to live by those words, and so very thankful that my mother didn't ask for more than that. I could keep seeing Madeleine and my mother in those holes the carrots left, but I'd rather see them in the bright faces of flowers. I'm also thinking about Madeleine's New Year's candles, and I pray that "light perpetual," as we say in church, shines upon my mother and my friend, forever and ever. Amen.

CHAPTER 6

All Good Gifts Around Us

For an abundance of the fruits of the earth,
let us pray to the Lord. —Book of Common Prayer

My daughter Eliza is a committed "jammer"—when berries are in season she picks them and makes jam. One summer morning she nudged me to drop my other responsibilities and join her. (What column? And wasn't I supposed to be writing a book? Those could wait until winter, she assured me.) Then, like the rest of my family often does, she suggested that I don't really work anyway. I'm just playing with words, as James Michener said, because I like the "swing" of them "as they tangle with human emotions." She also suspected I wasn't writing at all, but emailing, or reading the *Juneau Empire,* the *Anchorage Daily News, Salon,* and the *New York Times* online. Which was half-true. Then she reminded me that I can't really be a writer since I can't type—I use only two fingers. "Come on, let's start jamming," Eliza coaxed, as she hummed Bob Marley's reggae tune.

Anne Morrow Lindbergh wrote that a mother at her desk is always interruptible for any reason at all, while a father in the same chair gets tiptoed around. Even though that was back before Betty Friedan, it's still true at our house. Although, when you get right down to it, I *want* to be interrupted. I love the distractions as much as I love the writing, and I'm certain I wouldn't have one without the other. I lost a whole summer of gardening and gathering the year I was run over, and I missed it terribly. I didn't want to see Paris in the springtime; I wanted to plant my garden. I didn't want to go out to dinner; I wanted to grill salmon on a campfire down on the beach in my backyard. Then, the only thing I still could do was to write, and it wasn't enough. I grew tired of my own company. There's that, and even though my column deadline was technically that afternoon, I knew I could email it first thing the next morning, which was what I'd do anyway, whether I sat at my desk or went berry picking.

Alistair Cooke produced his terrific and highly lauded *Letter from America* weekly radio column in a thoroughly organized, completely controlled way. As soon as he recorded one, he began writing the next, and he wrote and revised it for a few hours each day until it was due, and then he'd start all over again. He kept this up for fifty-eight years. I would like to tell you that this is how I write my weekly column for the *Anchorage Daily*

News, which runs on Thursdays and is due on Mondays (sort of) and which I have maintained for a little over ten years. But this is how I really do it: I try not to think about it for four or five days and then all day Monday I plan to have something written down — words, ideas, a list, anything — by dinnertime, which for some reason on deadlines often includes unexpected company. Before the dishes are washed, which my husband does since by then I have started to panic, I'm back at my desk. It's now about nine, and the column was due at five. This is not as terrible as it sounds. A few years ago I discovered that the editors at the *Daily News* didn't read what I sent them until the next morning, which gave me a whole extra night to fret. So, after dinner on Monday I sit down and write a story or an outline or even a letter I'll never mail to a friend, about what's going on in Haines or at our house, what I think about it, and maybe a bit of insight into what it means. It is usually awful and too long, and if I died writing it and anyone ever found it they would think my columns must have been ghostwritten. Last year I learned that no one at the paper really reads my column until closer to noon the day after it is due. So now I wake up at 4 a.m. Tuesdays, often delete everything I wrote the night before, and start again, simultaneously convinced that I will lose my job and be the laughingstock of the world when this gibberish is actually printed with my name on it in the paper *and* that what I have to communicate and the way I do it will win a Pulitzer Prize and no doubt earn me a MacArthur genius grant. Writing a column makes me completely bipolar.

On those deadline mornings, even though my desk is on the wide corner of the stair landing between the first and second floors and even though all of my children and my husband have to walk by me to eat breakfast, I don't greet them. Sometimes, I don't even hear them leave for work and school. I prefer to think that I am as focused as a downhill ski racer "in the zone." Chip has a different view. He points at me, typing away on two fingers, in my pajamas, with empty coffee cups and a week's worth of notes on my desk, where the candle of Nuestra Señora del Perpetuo Socorro (Our Lady of Perpetual Help) is not burning, since I never light candles except at dinner, because I might forget to blow one out and burn the house down, Chip points at me and says, "Kids, take a good look. This is your mother on crack."

But I don't care, because as much as I love my family and my children and this busy life, I need something more, something that is my own. I started writing because I could do it at home and because I heard good stories every day and, when I'd share one with a friend or my family, they would listen; and when I shared some idea I had or some thought about what this life may mean, they'd nod in agreement or laugh. That's why I write. Without my family and all the activity that swirls around us in this small Alaskan community, I might not have anything to say. After all, I don't write about space aliens, African detectives, or cowboys. When I read that E. B. White said that he preferred working at home to an office, because he did his best thinking to the ebb and flow of the living room tide, I knew exactly what he meant.

I was always aware that without my family life I would have no so-called career. But my daughter J.J. was the one who reinforced that one winter when she was in junior high, at that age when one day you are twelve going on thirty and the next day you are twelve going on six. We had just returned from a trip back east. The airport screening had frightened her. There had been another school shooting in the news, and she was worried that it could happen in Haines. Normally steady J.J. had tears in her eyes when she said she didn't want to go to school. She was scared. That was a Monday, too, a "work" day. It was cold and clear and the ice on the pond was perfect. So she skipped school and I skipped writing and we walked up the snowy trail through the woods. Yes, they were lovely, dark, and deep—I bet Robert Frost discovered that on a walk in the forest when he was on a deadline, too. That's one benefit of deadlines: They imbue everything with new and very deep meaning. They make you pay attention. In that way, it is a spiritual practice.

Our vicar, Jan Hotze, tells us that God is all around us; the problem is we don't see Him because we are not looking. It's like that old joke, the one about a guy who is pulled out to sea by a bad undertow and prays for God to come rescue him. A kayaker paddles by and asks if he needs a hand. "No," he says. "The Lord is coming." A water-ski boat comes by, slows down, and asks if he's okay. "Fine," he says. "I'm waiting on the Lord." Finally a helicopter with a Coast Guard rescue swimmer on board hovers over him, and still he rejects the assistance, waving them off. So he drifts out into the ocean. It's getting dark and he prays like Jesus did. "Oh, Lord, why have you forsaken me?" The clouds part and God hollers down, "I sent a kayak, a motor boat, and a helicopter—what more can I do?" I like to think that deadlines inspire writing the way crises inspire prayer, but I hope that I'll recognize divine assistance when I see it.

The column that came out of the day J.J. and I skated all by ourselves until the low January sun went behind the mountains was that kind of gift. We two glided on a glassy pond deep in the woods, pretending we were ice dancers, singing "My Favorite Things" in alternating lines. She'd holler, "When the bee stings," and I'd shout, "When the dog bites," and then in unison we'd speed over the ice belting out, "And then I don't feel so bad." J.J has an unaffected clear soprano voice; she sings the national anthem at home basketball games. I can read music and carry an alto tune in the chorus but, as for solos, let's just say that what I lack in talent I make up for with enthusiasm. A remote pond is the best place for me to sing. By the time we hiked back down the trail, our bodies were tired and our hearts were light. We had done a few of our favorite things, J.J. really didn't feel so bad, and I had something sweet and timely to write about.

I hummed a little bit of "My Favorite Things" that summer morning and looked at my devotional candle, encased in a tall glass. On the front is a decal of the Virgin Mary, on the back a prayer, in Spanish and in English, that reads, in part, "Mother of good counsel . . . you come to my aid and my urgent needs and be my guide in all things. Blessed symbol of heart and home, may your love and charity for all God's children look favorable upon me." (If you read it with a Spanish accent it sounds perfect; the translation is a little bumpy.) When I ask Mary, as the mother of us all, to treat me well, I know that as the mother of only five I should be able at least to watch over my own home.

Summer days slip away faster than they used to. I appreciate them more because I came so close to not having any more summers at all. At an Episcopal burial service, Psalm 90 is usually read to remind mourners that our lives are as temporary as a summer field: "In the morning it is green, and groweth up; but in the evening it is cut down." My oldest daughter, Eliza, is done with college, the second is engaged, my son is in college, and the two younger girls are flying through high school. Sooner than I want, I'll have lots of time to write and not nearly as much to write about. In the meantime, Eliza was still standing behind me humming "Jammin'," and when I closed my laptop, she said happily, "I knew you'd come."

Last year Eliza picked gallons of blueberries for her jam. This year the blueberries are slow, or late, or hiding. It has been a funny fruit year that way. My two sweet cherry trees did not produce one cherry. The Yellow Transparent apple tree has three apples on it, but the little dwarf Rome apple tree, an experiment in this climate, is so loaded with fruit its branches are sagging. The garden strawberry plants were covered with berries and were eaten straight from the yard or on breakfast cereal. There were no leftovers for jam or the freezer. The wild strawberries nearby are off-limits because my neighbor Linnus has staked the patch as hers, although this year she couldn't do anything about the bear that raked them clean.

But the raspberries are another story. The abundant wild beach berries are small and sweet, the cultivated berries big and juicy. In lots of yards and alleys around town they have grown all mixed up with each other, making for a hybrid half-wild urban-style berry, or at least as urban as this small town gets. They grow by the sidewalks, along side streets, in vacant lots, and next to old sheds. The way Eliza and I look for them is to cruise slowly on our bikes watching for telltale red dots in the bushes. I was carefully riding a purposely clunky, heavy, English-style town cruiser. I had not yet braved a "real" ride, on a racing bicycle. My accident taught me two critical and literal lessons about bicycles and automobiles. The first is that when you are cycling on a road with cars, pretend you are invisible; assume the drivers cannot see you. The second is that if you are headed for a collision with a vehicle, don't try to avoid it and fall over off your bike and skid under it, as I did. Run into it and dive over the top. That way you may break an arm and a few ribs but will probably not die, or almost die. Of course, you should always wear a helmet. I had one on for the easy berry-picking ride, as we peddled and coasted, looking for the distinctive raspberry bush canes and leaves, and those spots of red.

We carried empty quart yogurt containers with strings attached to hang them around our necks, allowing us to pick with two hands. We had gallon freezer bags to dump the berries into when our cups were full. Three yogurt containers equal one bag. A full bag equals one batch of jam (about eight jars) plus a bowl of fresh berries for eating.

When you pedal a bicycle slowly, you see, hear, and smell things you might normally miss. I feel more awake, more aware somehow than I do at my desk, or even when I'm running errands in the car. When E. B. White was deep into the work of writing in the front room of his farm in Maine, his favorite break was to head down the road on his old Raleigh three-speed, because, he said, it helped "remove the cobwebs." I bet he edited those webs while he pedaled along and that during his daily ride he was able to see more in them than you or I would; he was, after all, some writer.

Searching for ripe raspberries is as much fun as finding them. There is a field across from the harbor, adjacent to the Presbyterian church, filled with big fat raspberry-bearing bushes. Some had been planted there when the clearing held a large garden and a small herd of dairy cows, a hundred years ago, back when the missionaries also ran an orphanage and a school on the same site. As soon as it became apparent that this was a magical year for the old raspberry bushes, we hardcore berry gatherers tried to keep the news of the bumper crop quiet, in part (forgive me, Lady of Perpetual Help) so there would be more for ourselves. The other concern was that we weren't sure it was okay to pick them. It might be stealing.

That is the only problem with harvesting berries in town. The ground they grow in usually belongs to someone. These berries were, technically, the Presbyterians'. My friend Lisa solved this moral dilemma by inviting a Presbyterian Sunday school teacher to come pick with her. She also reasoned that if they are church berries, then they are God's berries and therefore all mankind's, "which means us too, right?" And what's more, she added, "There are so many we can't pick them all, anyway, and no one wants them to go to waste." My plan was to pick as much as I needed without asking permission and then bring Pastor Ron Horn and his wife a jar of jam to thank them. This is an old Alaskan tradition when it comes to our always contentious land-use issues; it's known as "act now, ask later."

While we picked, hidden behind bushes taller than we were or crouched down among the shorter stalks, we heard the sounds of the summertime town: the drone of the harbor ice machine, the boats tying up at the fuel dock, the fishermen laughing and occasionally swearing loudly. We eavesdropped on conversations taking place down the gentle bank on the sidewalk. A few tourists off a cruise ship took the path that skirts the field from the harbor to the Visitor Center and stopped to ask what we were doing. When we told them, they asked how we knew the berries were edible. They were suspicious of berries that came right off bushes, of wild fruit that hadn't been washed or wrapped in cellophane at the store. When Ron opened his church office window to catch the breeze, I was afraid he might ask what we were doing as well, but he waved, which we took as a blessing. The smell of garlic from the lunch special at the nearby Lighthouse Restaurant signaled that it was time to leave. We'd been picking all morning and there was still a lot of boiling, sterilizing, and cooking to do before we had jam.

Once all the jars were hauled up from the cellar, checked for cracks and washed, and the new lids were sterilized, once everything was laid out, from measuring cups to funnels, and once the large speckled black and white enamel kettle was filled with water and the flame turned up high underneath it, Eliza and I crushed the berries in a cast-iron pot, added pectin and sugar, and let it all roll to a boil. Then we quickly and carefully poured that gorgeous, rich, red, seedy goop into hot, clean jars; screwed the two-part lids on them; lowered each one into a kettle of boiling water for ten minutes; and finally—gingerly but firmly—fished them out with the rubber-edged tongs designed for this purpose and set them on dishtowels on the counter. This is when I pray that the jars will seal, so that they'll keep safely all winter in the pantry and we can taste sunshine on a snowy day.

Sweat trickled under our shirts as Eliza and I arranged those half-pints of what seemed to be some kind of miracle in rows to cool down. When we had finished one batch—there were four more to go—I stepped out the back door to cool off myself. Through the open door I could hear the reassuring pop of lids sealing and Eliza washing the sticky pots and more jars and mixing up more berries and sugar, singing as surely as if she were a backup band member for Bob Marley and the Wailers.

The next morning, as I do every Tuesday, I sat down with my unlit candle and a strong cup of coffee with cream and wrote a column about making jam and picking berries and my daughter and some thoughts on the whys and what-fors of motherhood, too. I ate toast with the new jam on it, knowing that nothing I do at my desk could compete with homemade raspberry jam. It's the best work I do.

A FEW WEEKS LATER, I was confident that I would be prepared for the next column and had cleared my week to write a good one, at a reasonable pace, when I was sidetracked yet again. This time I had to move my laptop to the kitchen in order to keep an eye on two big polished aluminum pressure canners loaded with forty-eight half-pint jars of smoked salmon while they hissed and rattled on the stove like something from Franken-stein's laboratory. I watched them closely to be sure the pressure gauge didn't dip below eleven pounds, because then I'd have to start all over again and it had taken the better part of three days to get that far. Well, truthfully, I didn't go that far—just up the river for the fish and across the garden to my smokehouse.

For the next two hours I couldn't travel farther than five feet from the canner gauges. Because I couldn't leave the room, the kitchen was cleaner than it had been in weeks. I'd also already written a short obituary for the *Chilkat Valley News* in memory of a nice ninety-three-year-old woman who had lived here for ten years some thirty-five years ago and who no one could remember at all. I even called Clyde over at his seafood store, because he knew all the old-timers. "She was real nice," he said, but couldn't recollect anything specific. Tom will not let me use "She was real nice" in an obituary unless I can prove it and, although everyone else I called repeated the sentiment, that was all they could summon. This may be proof that being nice is not always the best policy. To make a lasting impression, you have to do more. The final call I had made was to the woman's elderly neighbor, who once more confirmed that our gal was nice but also could not think of one particular charitable act to illustrate it. So we talked instead about her own granddaughter, who was swimming in the Olympic trials that week.

THEIR OWN TWENTY-MILE swim up the river is why the salmon in my canners will taste different, some say better, and less oily, than the salmon Chip and I have caught in salt water. These fish came from a friend's net set in the river up in Klukwan. The Chilkat River hosts all five species of Pacific salmon, which is rare. We were after sockeye, whose dark red meat is best for smoking. There were a few king salmon still making their way upstream, so we were careful to let them go, in order to allow them to spawn for future fishing seasons. It was cool and breezy and threatening rain as we cleaned our catch on a weathered wood workbench with burlap tacked to it. The top sloped slightly toward the river, sluicing all the waste toward the water. The guts slid off the edge with a splash into the swift-moving current, to feed more fish and fertilize the soil for more berries. The river here is so full of glacial silt that it could be milky green paint. My future son-in-law, a fisheries biologist, has done studies that confirm the Chilkat River salmon know their way back to their natal spawning grounds by smell; the water has a kind of aroma, at least it does if you are a fish. To me, it smells like summer and, in addition to going a whole one without gathering berries after my accident, I had also missed canning salmon. I wasn't going to lose any opportunity. This domestic therapy was as important to my recovery as physical therapy.

Which is why the whole house smelled of smoke and salmon and the shot of vinegar in each canner that keeps the jars sparkling. It's the smell of harvest time and of a kind of love. That brings me full circle as well, to the ebb and flow of the tide in my kitchen. I was listening to those canners rattle, thinking about Presbyterian berries—I have read recently that scientists now believe the Milky Way has an odor, too, and it contains a chemical that gives raspberries their flavor—and also of something else E. B. White wrote about life on his farm, the one that gave him eggs and butter and the inspiration for *Charlotte's Web*. He advised that when you enter a barn, remove your hat. The same could be said for a berry patch or smokehouse. And even though Thanksgiving was months away, I heard that old hymn, "We thank thee then O Father, for all things bright and good / The seed time and the harvest, our life, our health, our food." It ends so perfectly I wish I'd written it: "All good gifts around us are sent from heaven above / Then thank the Lord, O thank the Lord for all his love."

CHAPTER 7

You Are Going to Get Well

Let the whole world see and know that things
which were cast down are being raised up.
—Book of Common Prayer

I would like to turn back the clock and start this week over again. The second time around there would be no young people's late-night party, no drinking, no driving, and no one would be in a casket or in jail. I would not be at a funeral in the high school gym filled with grief-stricken friends and neighbors of both young men. And I do mean stricken. Sometimes it is not a cliché; most of the kids looked like they had been hit in the chest with a two-by-four.

I would not have had to witness a young man crumble as he tried to give the eulogy for his best friend, or read the essay that was written by the dead boy when he was fourteen and carried in his mother's wallet ever since. "There are lots of reasons people under twenty-one shouldn't drink alcohol. When kids drink, it puts a damper on what they could have been." That's what he had written six years ago.

I would not have had to listen to the same carpenter I'd heard swearing and laughing through the bushes while he was building a garage next door choke, "I loved that kid," or listen to the high school science teacher say of the dead boy, "The first time I laid my eyes on him I knew—there's a smart one. You could tell just by looking in his eyes. They had mischief, quickness, and intellect." In my revised version of this week's events, the ambulance call at 3 a.m. seven days ago would have been because old Mr. Aukerman's hip popped out—again.

If I could time-travel, I'd go to that party myself and take all the car keys and throw them deep in the raspberry bushes, and I bet every mother in town would come with me and lock arms to surround that home so no one could leave.

But we are too late now.

Instead, we listened to the foreign yet familiar words of the ancient Tlingit crying songs. Instead, we heard Mayor Jan Hill announce, "There's no other place in the world that comes together like this community does in a crisis." Jan is the aunt of the boy who died and, without children of her own, was as close to him as an aunt could be. Maybe even closer, since in Tlingit culture this relationship is very tight. While she is right—of course she is—I would really rather we not keep finding it out this way.

After the service, the crowd walked in the cold gray afternoon to the cemetery in a completely silent parade, right down the middle of the road on that long mile from the school to the graveyard, behind the slow-moving pickup bearing the boy in a box. I wish I had not seen the father of the young man in the casket put his arm around the mother of the kid who put him there and walk along with her. If I could, I would even erase that brave and holy act of mercy and wrench back the days, hours, minutes, and seconds of the hands on the clock of fate or chance or destiny or stupidity or whatever you want to call it, and begin this week over again. Then one boy wouldn't be in the cemetery and another wouldn't be in jail, destined for prison. As my mother would have said, "There but for the grace of God go we all."

THE BIG SUBURBAN was full of partying young people, nice kids from old Haines families, which is to say that they were connected to nearly everyone in town in one way or another, when it went off the road in the wee hours of a September morning, at the turn by the freight transfer company, on the 5K running route that the high school cross-country team calls the town loop. The speed limit there is 25 mph. We must have just missed it, someone must have been running to call the ambulance by the time I was driving a few blocks away, on empty streets under a huge full moon, to the ferry terminal to catch a boat south to a meet with the running team that I coach.

The volleyball team and their coaches were on the same ferry. At least two families had driven by the wreck and flashing lights on their way to the terminal. They said it didn't look good. Another witness said they heard someone was being medevaced to Juneau. That meant it might not be too bad: the lifesaving flights usually fly right over Juneau straight to Seattle.

But that hadn't been the case. The next afternoon, before we arrived in Sitka, we learned one boy was dead from injuries sustained in the crash, and the driver had been drinking and was charged with manslaughter. I had to tell the girls and the boys traveling with me that one of their friends or relatives was dead, and another of their friends or relatives was being held responsible. Everybody was crying for both boys. The driver is a friend of our family's who ran on my team when he was in school. My older daughters worked as deckhands on his fishing boat. The young man killed was also their friend and someone we knew and liked. It may be hard to believe with the universal cell service most places have, but two short messages were all that came through to the ferry in those hours, one from a teen in town relaying what had happened and another from my husband confirming it. The purser let us use the ship-to-shore phone line so the Suburban driver's little sister could make that painful connection home. Months later the young man at the wheel would be sentenced to fifteen years in an Arizona prison. (Due to a lack of space in Alaska, many of our prisoners are sent out of state, making the incarceration even more difficult since it's harder for families and friends to visit and support them.) It is hard to breathe when something like this happens; it can make you so weak you can't stand. The Tlingit crying songs at the funeral helped, and I was glad I was home from our meet in time for it.

Tlingit people believe that the ancient laments release the grief so it can't steal the breath of the mourners, especially a mother, wife, or aunt. The songs also appeal for the assistance of all the family and friends now in the spirit world. First, before I go any further, a disclaimer is in order. I have enough understanding of Tlingit culture to know that this is where I must apologize in advance for any mistakes I may make interpreting it and for unintentionally offending anyone. Throughout this story and others still to come, I have been very careful to be as accurate as I can and have checked with my Tlingit friends, the local museum, and texts on Tlingit culture and language, but I am by no means an expert. I am a neighbor, an admirer, and, I hope, a sharp observer. I'm sharing these events and customs with you not because I know them better than anyone else but because they moved me and because they helped heal my friends and me. Also, knowing about these Tlingit traditions just may make you stronger in the places that you didn't know you were weak. That said, I now think that by singing the crying songs, my Alaska Native neighbors and those of us who sort of hummed along in that crowded school gym called on all the Tlingit ancestors to reach out from the clouds, the sea, the rivers, trees, rocks, and ice—the ground we walk on and the earth we buried that boy in—to catch our song of sorrow on the exhale and hold on to it tightly, keeping it with them, so that the survivors would be able to inhale life-giving air. History helps the crying songs do their magic as well, since the same tunes and lyrics have been sung for centuries. There is a kind of cold comfort in knowing that terrible things happen in each generation, in every tribe or clan, in every community or family, and that for thousands of years, across time and terrain, human beings have survived them, and that most of us still wake up just about every morning with the hope that this day will be a good one.

AUSTIN HAMMOND, THE late chief of the Chilkoot tribe, once blessed a cross-country running team I coached by reminding us that the souls of our ancestors would be pushing up on the bottoms of our feet as we ran to make the race easier. I always think about that when I run with the team in Sitka's Totem Park, and of all the spirits of all the people who have walked and run the paths for a hundred years. They are so close I can feel them, not just with my feet, but in my still-healing bones. Something about the place makes me whisper, even when I'm coaching kids there. Totem Park is officially called Sitka National Historical Park. It was dedicated in 1910, but its trails and woodlands have been popular since the 1890s and the area has had local significance since 1804, when there was a bloody battle for Sitka between the local Tlingits and the Russian sailors who helped protect the then capital city of Russian Alaska. The park begins at the end of the sidewalk on the edge of downtown. It is 113 forested acres with wide, well-drained, sandy dirt paths winding through shaggy hemlocks, giant Sitka spruce trees, and fifteen equally, if not more, imposing totem poles. It is usually wet there, and often misty.

It was raining hard when my team did a practice run at the three-mile race course looping through several of the park's trails and over a wooden footbridge spanning a salmon-spawning stream, ripe with rotting fish. Talk about hard to breathe—the stench made our eyes water. This September morn my shoes and socks were so cold and wet that even my good foot was numb. The cross-country team and our community, like the kids in that wrecked Suburban, are made up of Tlingits, part-Tlingits, and the children or grandchildren of modern Alaskan pioneers. In this way we are not so different from the people who fought on both sides of that battle in this park all those years ago.

I wanted to tell the team that their history and culture should give them strength and wisdom. I hoped to say something inspirational, wise, and good, so they'd remember my words as I had Austin Hammond's. I decided to tell them about the Tlingits who survived the Battle of Sitka and ran back into the dense woods and steep mountains on Baranof Island all the way to Peril Strait, a wilderness trek that even today, with modern hiking gear, plenty of food, and a GPS device, is hugely difficult and rarely done. I would remind the kids that these totem poles and the park itself are perfect examples of beauty born of pain, of both the natural world and humankind's ability to transform tragedy into splendor. The problem was that I couldn't articulate all of that without sounding more Hallmark than Yeats. I wished I were a poet right then.

I also wanted to tell my runners that a good reason to stay fit and strong is in case they ever have to race for their lives the way the Sitka Tlingits had, or the people in the World Trade Center on another September day, or the von Trapps, that singing family from *The Sound of Music* who trotted over the mountains to escape the Nazis. I wanted to remind them to get in shape and stay there, so that if they, too, are ever hit by a truck, they might have the strength to survive it.

I was focused on putting these thoughts all together in a hopefully-not-too-trite word package to deliver before the next day's meet, when everyone suddenly stopped short in front of a perfect bright green lawn in the middle of the dark woods. The site of the Tlingit fort that was attacked by the Russians is oddly out of place among the trees, ferns, and devil's club bushes of the northern rainforest. A friend who had lived in Sitka told me that the grass was the killing field during the battle. She said it was so saturated with blood that trees could never grow there again. I have not found that story in any of the park literature, so it may not be true. But I hope it is, because I want to believe that nature is not always indifferent to our suffering, that something in this ground or the cedar logs used for the totem poles keeps our pain.

Before I could share that story or any wise thoughts at all, the team took off back down the trail. It was raining so hard they needed to keep moving or they'd get hypothermia, or at least a bad cold. I hobbled along as fast as I could but didn't catch them until they had run out of the park, past the last totems, the hundred-year-old cottages lining the street, the arts-and-crafts-style buildings of Sheldon Jackson College, the old yellow-planked Russian Bishop's House, past the crowded boat harbor, through a busy downtown intersection with Sitka's lone stoplight, and into a steamy Subway sandwich shop—the only place to take seventeen drenched and sweaty teens for lunch. We had jogged through two hundred years in three blocks. No wonder I was having trouble distinguishing between the past and present.

That night, I lay tucked inside my sleeping bag on the floor of a Sitka High School classroom listening to the kids breathing in their sleep. I wondered if I could pick up ringworm from the mats they had given us to soften the floor—they had previously been in the wrestling room. And why were there no windows? I was breathing in everyone's exhalations. I was also thinking that maybe I was getting too old for this public sleeping. When that happens, I'll have to quit coaching. Group camping on ferries and in schools is part of team sports in southeast Alaska. All the schools are separated by the waters of the Inside Passage, so we travel by ferry or plane to away meets, staying in the host community, sometimes in homes, sometimes in schools or churches, overnight if the ferry schedule and weather cooperate but more often for two or three days. Some trips lately have taken us a week. The ferry ride to Sitka alone lasted thirty-six hours.

And there I lay, breathing used air and feeling imaginary ringworms burrowing in my neck, and thinking some more about what I'd say in the morning before the race. Then I said my prayers, with a longer list of people to bless than usual at the end, since I included every runner and at least one former runner.

It was still raining when we jogged from the school to the park to warm up and stretch the next morning. Before the race began I spoke to the team. I said to run like a Tlingit warrior, like a Russian sailor, like a Sitka black-tailed deer. I told my young runners to be grateful— very, very grateful—for spirits past and present, for strong legs and good hearts and the mud on their shoes and sweat in their eyes, for each other, for this place and for all the blessings of this life, especially for the rain on their sweet, wet heads right now. That's the best advice I could give them. The totems and trees, the rotting salmon and their eggs buried in the silt until next spring, would have to give the rest of this lesson.

A FEW WEEKS LATER I was back in Sitka again, for the raising of a new totem pole on the other side of town from Totem Park. This was not a copy of an old pole or a traditionally themed modern pole. It was a different kind of pole. In the old days there were four main styles of totem poles: crest poles depicted the story of a family ancestry; history poles told the story of a clan or group of families; legend poles documented important cultural tales that shouldn't be forgotten; and memorial poles were carved when someone died, and often contained the ashes of their subject. The collection in Totem Park was there because, in 1905, the then governor for the District of Alaska, John Green Brady, placed the poles in the popular town park, among the trees and trails, much as they still are today. Governor Brady had collected the totems from several villages in southeast Alaska with the help of what was left of the local Native leaders and the Coast Guard. At the turn of the century many of the once-thriving Native communities were ghost towns, thanks to the introduction of civilization by fur and fish traders and missionaries: Western diseases and alcohol wiped out whole tribes and, after that, much of what remained of tribal life was destroyed in the name of God.

Governor Brady himself played a part in this near extinction. He had been a street kid in New York City when he was taken in by the Children's Aid Society and sent west on an orphan train to adoptive parents in Indiana. The Greens (thus his middle name) sent him to Yale and Union Theological Seminary. He ended up a Presbyterian missionary in Sitka of all places, which was by then no longer the Russian, but now the American, capital of the Alaska district. The Reverend Brady believed God had found the Greens and they had saved him from a life of crime. He also believed that the Alaska Natives he preached to could be similarly saved if they became "civilized" — that is, baptized, educated, dressed, and housed like good Presbyterian Americans. He did his best to accomplish all of this. And his best was pretty good, or bad, depending on your point of view. He advocated removing children from their parents and villages to be schooled in Western ways; banning large celebrations, or potlatches; denouncing Native shamans, or spiritual leaders; and prohibiting the speaking of the Tlingit language as well as Native songs and dances. He was pleased with how well his converts assimilated. He believed he could save more Native souls if he built more residential schools and orphanages and had even more books, medical supplies, clothes, and food. The church and government leaders back east, though, did not support him. They wouldn't spend any more money on his mission. Also, even after his Native students were educated and dressed in American clothes, the local authorities would not let them attend public schools, which angered him.

So the Reverend Brady quit missionary work and became a trader, buying and selling, among other goods, Native art and curios. I'm sure there was much more to his exit from church work, but that is all the history I could find. Later, he was appointed judge and served as governor. As a missionary, he would have approved of the church ban on the carving of new totem poles. Yet as governor he collected them and preserved them in what I think must be the most beautiful and reverent setting in the world. I prefer to think that he came to feel guilty about his role in their near demise and that he had a change of heart toward the people who carved them, but that may not be accurate. He may have simply appreciated the way they looked. My Native friends might say that it was the power of the spirits in the poles, and all around them, that moved Governor Brady, whether he knew it or not. I do know that when you walk in Totem Park today and see where Governor Brady set the poles (some are now replicas, as the originals have been moved inside to protect them from the elements) and how the light filters down through the spruce boughs, catching the ovoid eye or the hook of a beak or the spring of a totemic bear, you know there's much more to them than wood and paint. You can feel it.

A hundred years after Governor Brady saved what he thought were the last totem poles in the world, it was time to raise a new one, and I was helping. This pole, like all poles, has a name. It is *Yei eek kwa neix* in Tlingit, or "You Are Going to Get Well" in English. It was carried about four blocks in the relentless Sitka rain, from the tent it was carved under to the front of the Southeast Alaska Regional Health Consortium Community Health

Services Building (the consortium is called SEARHC but pronounced "Search"), on a campus that includes the Mt. Edgecumbe public boarding school for rural high schoolers, a hospital, and a drug and alcohol treatment center. The Native-run nonprofit organization operates clinics in most southeast Alaska communities, including the new one in Klukwan, the village about twenty miles north of my house, and the old one in Haines. In 1975, sixteen Tlingit women, many of them grandmothers, all but one from small villages, formed the consortium to provide better Native and rural health care. (By *small villages* I mean ones with fewer than 1,000 residents; Klukwan has about 150.) These women didn't hold a grudge. From the beginning they decided that their clinics would serve non-Native people, too. SEARHC is so successful it has replaced the Indian Health Service in southeast Alaska. The consortium's board of directors remains mostly Tlingit grandmothers and *aunties,* a Native term of endearment and respect. They have recently added dental care to their clinics, so that their grandchildren won't be shy about smiling.

WAYNE PRICE HAS A SMILE as wide as a river and as bright as a full moon. He designed this new totem pole, carved it, and supervised others who also worked on it as part of a project funded by SEARHC called *Kootéeyaa,* or "Journey to Wellness." Wayne has declared this a new kind of totem pole. He says it doesn't tell a story, illustrate

history, or memorialize a person but, rather, is designed
to heal. In keeping with Tlingit tradition, he asked the
elders permission to carve it and their guidance in raising
it properly. Native people believe that you can't just stick
a totem pole any old place, any old way. There are proper
songs, proper prayers, proper thank-yous, and proper gifts
that go with the raising. The Tlingit people pay as much
attention to honor and tradition—or maybe more—than
the British royal family.

While Wayne maintains that this pole splits with the
past in many ways, I'm not sure the new pole is that far
removed from the ones standing in the nearby park. After all, Wayne's carving really does tell a story, illustrate
history, and memorialize Tlingit women such as the
ones who founded SEARHC. The act of carving it is the
tale of both Wayne's trip from drinking to sober and of
Tlingit survival. It's about his mission to help others—
especially Native men—heal what ails them through
culture, art, and Native American spirituality. It's pretty
simple: "Carving saved my life," Wayne says.

Wayne has lived hard but managed to produce a lot of
great art in spite of it. He has more than two dozen totem
poles to his credit. His silver and wood carvings are in
many villages in southeast Alaska, as well as in galleries
and museums around the state and around the country.
One of Mary and Warren Price's eleven children, he grew
up in Haines, lost three brothers to untimely or accidental
deaths, and has been married and divorced. A son, Steven,

named after one of his dead brothers, was there to help that day. Cherri, the woman he calls his soul mate and who would soon be his new wife, was also there, with her son. Jeremy, whom Wayne dotes on, is restricted to a wheelchair as a result of his difficult birth. Now a teenager, he can't speak words, walk, or eat on his own. But he does understand everything you say. He laughs and makes other people laugh. He listens to books on tape. Later that night at the celebration potlatch for the pole raising, as tradition and the elders dictate, Wayne would perform a carver's dance, in full Tlingit regalia, with sealskin moccasins on his feet, a red and black felt button blanket over his shoulders, a painted wooden hat tied on his head, and the black and white woven pouch of carving tools hanging from his belt. Then, he would lift Jeremy out of his wheelchair, holding him in his arms as gently as Mary cradled Jesus in the Pieta, and they would dance and dance while the skin drum beat, Native voices chanted, and the rest of us bore witness in silent awe.

Jeremy is well on the inside; it's his outside that causes him trouble. With Wayne, it has often been the opposite. At forty-nine he is strong and clear-eyed, but for much of his life he followed a pattern typical of the so-called boom and bust days of his Haines youth. From long-shoring—Wayne and his father loaded lumber ships for the sawmill—to commercial fishing, logging, and carving cedar with some of the region's great totem pole carvers at the Haines nonprofit Alaska Indian Arts, the pattern was the same: work really hard and play even harder. Sweat, then party. That was how many Alaskan guys lived, it's how many still do, and it's why we keep losing them.

We almost lost Wayne, too, who at one low point realized that he "couldn't just put a cork in the bottle" and go off to carve another pole. He had to walk away from the drinking and drugs for good. He had the vision for what he sometimes calls the "wellbriety" pole shortly after that, in a sweat lodge in the lower forty-eight where he went to steam the poisons out of his body. He didn't just see the design—he even had a vision about the wood chips that would fall from his adz while he carved it. Wayne's ancestors' spirits told him that each chip would represent a soul lost to alcohol, drugs, HIV, violence, poverty, and even war. They were pretty talkative spirits.

Here is the design Wayne saw in that steamy vision and later carved: A raven is on top of the pole, because in Tlingit lore Raven created the world. Next comes the shaman or priest or, some would say, medicine man. He has the power to heal the body and soul and to see and hear what other people can't. (Wayne said his pole was the first one to defy Governor Brady's—and others'—long-ago ban on listening to shamans and honoring their role in Tlingit culture.) The wolf is next, because in Wayne's sweat-lodge vision a wolf ran back into the dark places of addiction, persecution, illness, and violence, and with the determination of an EMT crawling through the window of an overturned Suburban, used his teeth to drag the

ailing person out into the light. The woman below the
wolf figure represents the mother of us all. In Tlingit culture, family lines are traced through the mother's side.
"It's the women," Wayne reminded his helpers, "who
hold our people together."

Just like Tlingit mayor Jan Hill did that September day
when she officiated at her nephew's funeral in the Haines
High gym.

When visitors came to the carving tent while Wayne
was working, he invited them all, from camera-pointing
cruise-ship passengers to homeless drifters, to write a
name on a wood chip and place it into a special pile. A
student from a tiny interior Alaska Native village attending the Sitka boarding school wrote names on twenty
chips. Can you imagine that kind of sorrow? A teenager
with that much grief? The chips were like crying songs
you could hold on to.

BUT I WAS ABOUT to pick up and hold on to
something much larger. We were all there to literally lift
the pole and carry it to its new permanent home. I looked
at the wet wood of Wayne's finished carving as it lay on
its back on sturdy sawhorses in the rain. From the shiny
metal ring in the raven's beak at the top to the raspberry-
painted toenails of the strong woman on the bottom, it is
a wonder. The larger-than-life-sized woman at the base is
a first, as traditional totem poles featured men. She must
be eight or ten feet tall. And despite the old saying "low

man on the totem pole," the figure on the bottom of a Tlingit pole holds a place of high honor; some carvers say the highest honor. A Native man next to me touched the woman's muscular cedar arm and said, "It's a Tlingit David."

We were an interesting crowd, about half Native and half non-Native, including artsy types from Sitka, doctors and staff from the SEARHC health centers, fishermen, teachers, addicts and recovering addicts, clergy, Wayne's family and friends from Haines and Klukwan, and even some sailors from the nearby Coast Guard base, the moral descendants perhaps of Governor Brady's totem-moving crew. When Wayne realized how heavy the pole was, and how difficult it would be to move, he contacted the fire department. The guys were happy to help, but since they were technically on a call they were required to wear full firefighting gear. There were also a lot of wet dogs and little children splashing in the puddles and running around in the rain. Roberta Kitka, one of those SEARHC women leaders I told you about, remained dry and serene under her broad umbrella. There was no mud at all on her immaculate outfit that was all red and black, the colors favored by Tlingit artists, and accented with carved totemic-designed silver jewelry. She told me she had labored for years to help Wayne "give birth" to this project. Looking at the pole, she whispered, "It makes chills run up and down my spine."

Well, it made shooting pains run up and down mine. I

hoped my pelvis repairs would hold. I had figured our help was going to be largely ceremonial. I thought a couple of front-end loaders would actually move the pole. Wayne didn't. He had faith that we could lift, carry, and raise it ourselves. He didn't have a backup plan, or even a safety net of any kind. If we dropped it, we'd have to pick it up; if we broke it, we'd have to repair it; if we couldn't carry it, it wasn't going anywhere. Not only that, but everything was cold, wet, and slippery. Still, Wayne and Roberta and all the SEARHC grandmothers and aunties wanted the world to know that it's going to take some heavy lifting by many people to heal what ails Tlingit culture.

Which, judging from what happened next, is in pretty good shape to begin with. About 140 people gathered four deep on each side of eighteen four-by-fours and used them to lift the forty-one-foot long four-thousand-pound cedar totem pole and carry it from the shelter it was carved in, down the street, and to the lawn it would stand on. Wayne was a lot calmer than my husband, Chip, is when he pulls our twenty-eight-foot sailboat out of the water, and we use a truck and a trailer. Wayne had his crew—half a dozen Native men with red bandanas tied around their necks to identify them—hand out white knit fishing gloves to help us grip the wet four-by-fours. We found our places as someone down in the front yelled to Wayne, who was standing on a sawhorse, "How are we supposed to lift it? With our forearms or hands? Or what?"

"With all your heart," Wayne said.

He didn't say then that this was the heaviest pole he'd ever worked on; it had uncharacteristically required block and tackle to shift it during the carving. Wayne believes that the extra weight in the wood is from the heavy burdens it absorbed from people who visited it and worked on it during the carving. For six months, healing circles met daily at the carving tent, plus all those folks in all kinds of trouble who came to the pole to touch it and cry or pray or tell it their stories and sign a memorial wood chip. Mayor Hill, who is also the president of the SEARHC board these days, said earlier that she was drawn to the pole by its healing powers. She said being near it made her feel better about her losses. While I was lifting the pole, I saw her at the edge of the crowd. She was recovering from a broken ankle; her foot was in a boot cast. She couldn't join us lifters, but she was watching us from underneath an umbrella. Maybe she was thinking about the husband she had lost to cancer and about the nephew she had lost in that tragic car wreck. No doubt she would have liked them to be part of this. When our eyes met, there was a jolt like a shock. I didn't know her well enough to know how to react, it felt so personal. Maybe I was imagining it, but it was as if we were thinking the same thoughts, about the same spirits.

Wayne broke the spell with a shout: "One, two, three, lift!" And the pole lurched up. I was grateful for the burly firemen on either side of me. There is no way we are going to move forward, I thought. But we did, slowly, to the beat of a skin drum and the chanting of Tlingit songs. These were not crying songs. These were working songs, happy songs; they were more like rowing songs. From above we must have resembled some kind of Viking ship. We shuffled forward and made it past two of the houses on the slick rainy street before sawhorses were tucked underneath the pole. We lowered it gently on Wayne's command and shook out our arms, stretched our backs, and adjusted sopping wet rain gear. I pulled off my hood. There was no point—I was soaked and it only made it harder to see and hear.

When we began again my arms trembled. I thought of Wayne's stories about the pole taking the weight from people and decided to give it some of my worries. All around me I could feel, or thought I could feel, people doing the same thing. I'm not sure if it worked but I know that after the break, our movement was much easier. I felt stronger. The pole was lighter. Maybe we had mastered the awkward lifting and shuffling motion. Or maybe, because Wayne and Roberta and all the people around me believed it could heal, the pole did. Maybe by carrying it and sharing its story and its load, we brought out the power we already had to heal ourselves.

I couldn't think more about that then, though, because we had to pivot—that's right, all 140 of us and that two-ton pole had to turn off the road and step up an eight-inch curb and slog across the grass to the place where we would plant it forever. What used to be a lawn quickly mashed into boot-sucking muck. We slipped, and the pole slid on the four-by-fours. Luckily its weight made any movement very slow. Wayne yelled, "Whoa," and we regrouped, steadying the pole.

Behind me a petite frizzy-haired blonde woman wearing a wet fleece beret said, "Now we know how Stonehenge got there." A tall Native man in yellow rubber rain gear next to her replied in a guttural Tlingit accent, "We're not there yet."

Wayne and his crew directed us to tilt the bottom end of the pole in the hole already dug for it and, using sawhorses and blocks of wood to brace it, we raised the top end about eight feet before setting it down so Wayne could tie six long ropes around it with towels padding the contact points to protect the carving and paint from chafing. The two in the front were tossed over a lashed log crossbar Wayne had built for this purpose. The other ropes led from it to the back and sides. The elders, dressed in red, black, and blue button blankets and wearing ceremonial wooden hats and holding carved staffs, said a Christian prayer and sang a Tlingit song and dropped two coins into the hole: a "wellbriety" token and Sacagawea dollar.

The rain finally quit as Wayne cued the front lines, and the crowd, which was standing so close together that we were all touching, leaned back into each one, slowly, sort of like in a tug-of-war. The two side lines were pulled taut in the same way, to keep the pole balanced as it rose. The back lines were held tight, too, in case we got too eager and pulled it up past the center point and tipped it over forward.

Then, the pole rose a few feet, swayed above the blocking, and stopped. The raven on top pointed heavenward. A live eagle perched on a nearby telephone pole sang her encouragement. The Tlingit people believe—and their tradition requires—that all actions are reciprocated. I'll tell you more about that later. Now you need to know only that the real eagle calling to the carved raven on the pole was a very good sign, a proper sign. Wayne noticed; so did the elders, and so did anyone paying attention, which was most of us.

Of course, we all knew it was a blessing. Some of us believed the eagle's encouragement was what finally raised the raven-crowned pole. But like most actions that rely on faith, it still took plenty of our own muscle and ingenuity. I watched, then, as Wayne looked away from the calling eagle with a nod and hollered, "Pull harder!" The black wooden raven with the brass (stars), copper (sun), and aluminum (moon) ring flashing in its beak soared up and over our heads. It felt as if the pole were raising itself.

Wayne ran back and forth, signaling for slack or tension in our lines, until guided by sight and a plumb bob, he pronounced the pole upright and true. A dozen men grabbed nearby shovels, and, working as fast as they could while we all held on tight to the lines, filled the hole with rocks, mud, and gravel. There was no concrete to be poured, no steel bar reinforcing the pole, no wires supporting the anchor, just an eight-foot tongue of wood below the bottom of the carving.

How will it stay up?

Wayne trusted the old carvers who did it this way for hundreds of years, allowing the weight of the pole to secure itself. Or at least he hoped the old guys were right. He instructed us to ease the ropes but not let go and to be prepared to pull hard again in order to catch the pole if it didn't stand on its own. The totem pole was so tall, so massive, so heavy, and so beautiful it was hard to believe we had just put it up there, harder still to believe it would stay. When the ropes slackened, though, it didn't even wobble.

It is a magnificent thing, inside and out, but even so, I would rather it hadn't been carved. I would rather Wayne and all of his ancestors had never needed to heal any pain at all. In the same way, I wished I had never seen the father of that dead young man put his arm around the mother of the young man who accidentally killed him. I wonder if to be human is to know that we can't ever banish pain and ugliness from the world, only learn from it and create something beautiful and good out of it—like the newest totem pole in Sitka, the one called "You Are Going to Get Well." If you ever see it, you will believe that's possible.

CHAPTER 8

Good Neighbors

Love one another
as I have loved you.
—John 13:34

O n Sunday, Nancy Nash played all the evangelical hymns, including every verse of "Amazing Grace." One former Holy Roller, as my mother would have called him, couldn't help raising his hands in praise. His faith was pulling on them with a spiritual force the opposite of gravity. He couldn't keep them down if he tried. This doesn't happen in most Episcopal churches, and rarely in ours. It has never happened to me, but while I used to snicker a bit at such open displays of faith, now I admire them. I know what Anne Lamott means when she says she may just slap one of those fish stickers on her car. (I have put a very small THE EPISCOPAL CHURCH WELCOMES YOU decal on mine.) This was also not the day to point out pet peeves with fellow worshippers. It was what I call

"Love Your Neighbor Sunday." The lessons and the sermon were the ones in which, Jan says, "the rubber meets the road."

This was the annual Sunday where we are reminded of the two rules that define our duty as Christians: loving God and loving our neighbor. All the rest are details. The Gospel reading was from John and included the story of Jesus giving his followers a new commandment: that we love one another as he has loved us. Expanding on that in her homily, Jan reminded us of the words those of us raised in the Episcopal Church used to hear at the beginning of every service (and that we sometimes still do). They're from the 1928 prayer book:

> Hear what our Lord Jesus Christ saith.
> THOU shalt love the Lord thy God with all thy heart, and with all thy soul, and with all thy mind. This is the first and great commandment. And the second is like unto it; Thou shalt love thy neighbor as thyself. On these two commandments hang all the Law and the Prophets.

It's pretty clear that if we all obeyed these commandments we would live peacefully and, most likely, happily ever after. The trouble is that while it sounds so simple, it is very hard to do. Especially when March comes in like a tsunami and goes out like a chicken.

A few days after the service, I was washing dishes and listening to a story on NPR about tourists finally returning to Thailand and Sri Lanka after the Christmas tidal wave a few years ago that killed about 225,000 people. It is hard to grasp that kind of grief. All those babies, old people, and even a little boy climbing a tree—all suddenly dead in the most traumatic of ways. You'd think that much loss on one day would forever alter the way the whole planet feels, in the same way forest fires affect global warming. You'd think it would trigger global keening.

I was also thinking of friends with cancer and heartaches, about the untimely death of another friend, and about Mother Nature, God, and Love, and why, if the soul of the universe is really good, any of this could be allowed to happen. I was pondering all of this when, through the window, I saw a black chicken leap off the fence into the white snow and sink softly out of sight. I pulled on my boots and coat and headed out to rescue her. She does this from time to time; so do her sisters. It's been a long winter and they are ready to explore the yard again. When I reached her she was down about a foot inside a hole in the snow, wings apart, not moving, not panicked at all—just floating there, looking up, waiting for me to rescue her, it seemed. I know chickens are not the most intelligent of creatures, but my hens have been raised to believe the world is good and that they are loved. She let me gently squeeze her wings to her sides, lift her up, and carry her back to the coop, setting her down on the sawdust in a burst of cackles and flapping. It made me happy to help her. But it was no trouble at all compared to how Mark Sebens truly helped after that terrible tsunami.

Mark traveled with a thirteen-member Christian medical relief team sponsored by the Crossroads Community Church in Palmer, a suburb of Anchorage, to Sri Lanka just twelve days after the disaster. Mark's wife, Jane, had heard about the trip from her sister, who is a member of the church, and her brother-in-law, a physician's assistant who also signed on for the mission. After looking at the news from Sri Lanka on television, Mark and Jane realized that her brother-in-law and his friends would need more than medical skill and goodwill to accomplish anything. They'd need someone who could keep a vehicle running, build a shelter, and wire electricity for their makeshift clinics so they could see to do the work they believed God had called them to do.

The *Chilkat Valley News* had run a story about the upcoming relief mission calling Mark a *Mad Max* kind of a guy. Volunteer firefighter Travis Reid declared Mark "a real life Alaskan MacGyver." Travis is the manager of the Chilkat Guides, a river-rafting company. He is as close as anyone comes to being Mark's boss. Mark keeps the Guides' buses and vans running. Mark works there because he wants to, and I have the feeling that if anyone gives him a hard time, he'll pack up his tools and leave.

I like to think of Mark as the good pirate of Lynn Canal. He listens to Jimmy Buffett and could be the subject of one of his songs. His sons are named Fletcher (as in

Christian of *Mutiny on the Bounty* fame) and Tristan (as in Jones, the more modern-day sailing adventurer and author with a lawless streak). Mark and his brother Tod (yes, it is just one *d*) have sailed the Caribbean and across the Pacific in funky boats. Once, they even threatened off real Mexican pirates with homemade bombs. Mark's cool black patch helps him look the part—he lost an eye in a nail-gun accident. So does the ancient wooden fishing boat, *Angela*, which he keeps down in the harbor. He is not a Johnny Depp sort of leading man. He's more like Humphrey Bogart on the *African Queen*, only better looking.

If you ask Mark how he would describe himself—you know, a carpenter, electrician, mechanic, welder—he'll say, "I'm a fabricator." He built his house high on the side of Mt. Ripinsky overlooking the Chilkat River valley. He used to own a boat shop and is a pyro-technician, too. He and Tod have put on a lot of our town's fireworks displays. When Walt Disney Studios made the movie *White Fang* in Haines, Mark was hired to do special effects. He was the one who figured out where to find the equipment needed to melt and pour the paraffin used to cover the twenty-five-yard indoor swimming pool with a layer of fake ice that the film's hero, played by Ethan Hawke, could walk on and then fall through.

I am always pleasantly surprised when I see Mark dressed up, like when he portrayed Captain von Trapp in the Haines production of *The Sound of Music* and Daddy

Warbucks in *Annie*. As we say around here, "He cleans up pretty good." And even though, at fifty-one, he is old enough to be the dad of most of his teammates, he remains one of the best softball players in town. How he hits and fields so well without the depth perception of two eyes, I don't know.

Jane called Mark's surprise inclusion in the church relief group providential. Mark didn't say much about it at all, except that he was tired of winter and ready for a change. Mark does have trouble staying in one place for too long. The day before he left, I talked to him in his shop over at the Chilkat Guides. He had a good idea of what he would need. "Living in Alaska sets you up for this kind of thing. I make stuff with whatever I have."

The trouble was he couldn't take all of his tools and equipment. Space and weight were limited by the airlines and the uncertain nature of the expedition. They had to be able to carry everything they needed. Mark could take only essentials. He was choosing the supplies and tools that would allow him to make what he needed when he got there, using Sri Lankan materials. So far he had a roll of electrical wire, a coiled rope, a saws-all, a hammer that doubled as a hatchet, three rolls of duct tape, two rolls of electrical tape, a portable water pump, a block and tackle set, a glue gun, a volt meter, a respirator, and a bag of cotton face masks. Mark hoped to buy a new headlamp and a suitcase-sized generator by the time he caught the ferry south to the Juneau airport that night. A senior at

Haines High who works as Mark's sidekick after school was busy wiring a string of portable lights. Our lumberyard had donated the materials but had an even closer connection to the disaster: Nishan Weerasinghe, one of the employees who is also a friend, has relatives living in Sri Lanka. He lost a twelve-year-old cousin when the Sunday morning wave hit the church where the family was worshipping. Nishan's father, Kumar, who lives in Seattle, volunteered to expedite passports for the Crossroads Community Church group, and Nishan provided Mark with the names and addresses of people who could help him once he arrived in Sri Lanka. All the Weerasinghes gave Mark some money as well, instructing him to use it however he needed.

Mark talked to me as he dug through a box searching for a tube of J-B Weld, which is used to glue metal together. "It's been like that all day—everyone wants to help." The insurance agent quickly put a policy together. The Salvation Army stationed a bell ringer at the grocery store, and the Presbyterian church donated the previous Sunday's collection plate. At the bookstore on Main Street there was information on the counter about ways to aid the tsunami victims and, like everyone else who heard about it, the owners contributed to Mark's send-off.

I asked Mark if he'd had a religious conversion; he was, after all, going to be working with a church group. He winked with his good eye, shook his head no, and then said in his gravelly voice, "Listen, Heath, even atheists want to help people." Of course, you don't have to believe in any God to be a good person, and sometimes the worst people behave terribly in His name. I imagined Mark talking to one of the doctors or nurses or even patients, as he wired up a fan and lights in a stick-and-canvas clinic amid the ruins and sorrow, speaking just like Bogey's Charlie did to Katharine Hepburn's Rosie. "I don't blame you for being scared, not one bit," Mark might say. "Nobody with good sense ain't scared."

A FEW DAYS AFTER Mark returned to Haines, we were sitting in the Bamboo Room restaurant. "Basically," Mark said, stirring a third spoonful of sugar into his coffee, "it was like a nuclear bomb went off. You either made it or you didn't." He meant that there weren't as many injuries as his medical team had anticipated. There were hardly any. In that way, it was like the World Trade Center attacks. "This woman said her chest hurt and asked if we could help. She had lost her husband, children, parents, and home. Her heart was broken. Sure it hurt," Mark said. "You bet it did, but we couldn't fix it." Not with all the duct tape in the world, I thought to myself. Mark worked for four more days on crowd control and assisting the nurses handing out medicine for people he thought had more emotional ailments than physical ones. He went to bed thinking he hadn't traveled nine thousand miles to keep people in orderly lines. The next morning, a

Sri Lankan pastor asked him if he and the doctors would be willing to help with construction of a refugee camp. He drove Mark to a twenty-acre site that was drier than most, on high ground between two rice fields, and asked him to make it into a temporary village for about 1,500 people as soon as possible.

It took Mark two weeks.

"I had a compass and a GPS, so I paced it off and laid out a grid, you know, for housing, latrines, and streets that wouldn't be too muddy," he said, moving our BLTs and coffee cups and unfolding his map, drawn to scale in a Sri Lankan camp by the light of a headlamp. He pointed out the features as he spoke. Much of it was common sense, he said, such as making sure human and food waste were kept away from the water source and figuring out how to make the most of limited fuel to generate necessary electricity. "Really, Heath, it's not rocket science. Anyone could do this." I listened to his words, looked at his map, and thought: Mark built a tent town almost as big as Haines. He made it out of scraps with minimum tools and a hodgepodge group of laborers who spoke several languages, none universally. Many had never built a birdhouse before. It was definitely not something *anyone* could do.

The area hit by the tsunami, the eastern shore of Sri Lanka, was a densely populated rural fishing region that had long been isolated from the rest of the country by its geography, religion, ethnicity, and years of conflict. The residents weren't the most popular people in the country, for sure. Three-quarters of Sri Lankans live on the west coast, speak Sinhalese, and are Buddhists. The minority Tamils inhabit the isolated east coast, where Mark was. They speak Tamil and are Hindu. Since the 1970s the notorious Tamil Tigers guerilla militia has led a battle for independence from the Sri Lankan government that has earned them worldwide terrorist status and left more than seventy thousand people dead and thousands more maimed and homeless. They have their fans, though, many of whom are expatriate Tamils who want a homeland of their own. In April 2009, one hundred thousand Tamils and their supporters marched in London to show support for the terrorist organization.

Maybe it's a good thing Mark didn't know much about Sri Lankan religion and politics before he went. Because he assumed they were gentle, friendly people, to him they were. Maybe that is why Jesus said loving one another is the most important thing we can do, and why we are still aspiring to follow that—because loving your neighbors makes them more lovable. In spite of their reputation for fierceness, the mostly Tamil people Mark met, including, he now thinks, some "pretty high up Tamil Tiger leaders" (he could tell by both the size of their weapons and their posse of guards) were helpful. "They were so appreciative. Everyone kept thanking us," he said.

• • •

I WAS THINKING ABOUT that conversation with Mark, as I went back to washing the breakfast dishes after rescuing the chicken, when out the window I spied yet another hen walking along the top of the coop fence. She paused, then leapt like a heli-skier or a jilted lover. I'm not sure what her motivation was. And it didn't matter. I hurried out to rescue her. Most of us will do anything for our pets. My neighbor Betty sewed a yellow vest for her dog, Bart, to make sure no one mistakes him for a bear and accidentally shoots him. Putting a foundering chicken back in the coop is much easier than pushing a drooly Newfoundland out the door, as Betty will attest. Bart weighs more than she does. Betty, who's older than my mother was when she died, is from Rhode Island. When she yells for her dog to come back home, it sounds like "Baa-at." While it's difficult to shove Bart out the door this time of year, once he makes his move from the porch to the yard, he tends to amble off into the nearby woods or up the thawing streambed. The vest Betty made him resembles a neon life jacket—so any hunter will see he's a really big dog, not a medium-sized bear.

Not that you are allowed to hunt anything in our neighborhood on the edge of town. You may shoot a gun here only to protect people or animals. I know this because I checked with the police recently, after a new family rented a house across the road and I discovered that their dog was as aggressive as Bart is gentle. It stalked and killed our pet rabbit. "That was your bunny? We thought it was wild," the woman said when I knocked on her door in tears. Charlie was white with pink eyes and orange spots. J.J. and Stoli had dyed his fur. He had been a house bunny and was even litter-box trained, but one summer, after a day playing in the yard, he hopped over to the chicken coop and decided to stay. He had lived the life of a free-range chicken ever since, winter and summer. Each evening Charlie returned to the coop with the hens. They roosted on the poles above the floor, and Charlie hopped up into one of the egg-laying boxes lined with straw.

When I bought a half-dozen more chicks last spring, Charlie climbed onto the broody box, a plywood pen with a wire mesh top and a lightbulb for heat, where the yellow fluff balls fresh from the post office lived until they were sturdy enough for the bigger, unheated space of the coop. Charlie sat on top of that screen and watched the chicks all day and all night. The chicks watched Charlie back. When chickens are very young, they imprint maternal qualities on the other animals or people they see. My old hens grew up thinking I was their mother. This flock believed Charlie was their mother. He was, as Charlotte the Spider would have written, some rabbit.

After it killed Charlie in cold blood, the new neighbor's lean, skittish husky, with wild yellow eyes, waited a few days and then came back and dragged off two of my beloved older hens. At least I think she did. When I went over there, this time they said they hadn't seen any of my chickens. Then they promised it wouldn't happen again.

The next day, I was in the kitchen when I caught the bad dog lurking by the edge of the yard. I ran outside and yelled for it to get away. My very favorite hen of all time, six-year-old Ella, was out pecking in the sticky muck between melting snow piles. She was a black Australorp that liked to be petted between her wings, ride in the car on a lap on the way to a science class at school, and nestle right down next to one of the sleeping dogs on the porch. She was the one hen that liked me so much she ran toward the house when I opened the door. "No, Ella, stay!" I yelled, but she didn't understand. She high stepped it right across the driveway to see me, and that evil dog grabbed her by the neck, shook her limp, and took off with her in its mouth. I couldn't even breathe from the horrible violence of it.

I was so sick and angry that I didn't notice how easily I ran to the neighbor's house or how I took their steps two at a time, just the way I used to do before my accident, but I didn't care about that. I rapped on the door, shouting that they must stop their dog from murdering my pets, or I'd kill it with my bare hands. The strangers stood there, staring at me, silent and shocked. The children were young and there were puppies on the porch.

"Do something!" I screamed. The mother, with a baby on her hip and another one hugging her skirt, mumbled that she was very sorry and would pay for my chicken. "Chickens," I roared. "And Charlie." The father appeared behind her. I told them both that money was not the point and sobbed, "How do you compensate for the loss of living things you love? They cannot be replaced."

After her husband ran off to catch the dog, the wife kept saying, "I am so sorry." I waved her off with breath-catching hiccups. "I don't care. Just please stop your dog from slaughtering my pets, or I'll blast it to smithereens." I ranted something like that. She said her dog couldn't help it, that she was part wolf. They had tried to tie her up, but she didn't like it. She promised that their boy, who looked about five years old, would keep better track of the dog.

I told her that "my boy," who at eighteen is really more of a man, is pretty good with a .22, and that if their dog was in our yard again, he'd shoot it and kill it. As I stepped away I swore that we'd drop that dog dead on its lousy, rotten, murdering part-wolf feet. On my way down her thawing ice and mud driveway, I hollered over my shoulder that if I had a loaded gun handy their dog would already be "history, hamburger, crab bait!" That dog would be deader than a doornail, deader than a coffin nail, deader than Marley's dead ghost. "I'll blast it to kingdom come," I yelled again for good measure.

"Except you don't know how to use a gun," Eliza reminded me when I was back in the kitchen, "and you'd never kill a dog." Eliza had graduated from college right after my accident and had come back to share in my care and the running of our household. While her sister Sarah took over the nursing chores, even giving me shots of blood thinners, Eliza helped with the younger kids, animals, and cooking. She also jumped in where I had left off, volunteering at the library and school, and coaching the cross-country team with our friend Liam. Then she went places I could never have gone, becoming a wilderness EMT and joining Fireman Al and the rest of the ambulance crew. She is earning a distance master's degree in elementary education and is hoping to teach in the Haines school. She is so pretty, so capable, and so wise for her years that I can't believe we are related. Eliza also knows I would never let Christian shoot a bad dog, especially one that could be closely followed by a good little boy trying to catch its collar.

After I washed my face and had a glass of water, Eliza said, "That certainly went well." It was something my mother would have said. So was her next observation. "They'll never get that dog under control and there's nothing we can do about it but keep a close eye on the remaining chickens." My mother would have added that I had "misplaced emotions," that this wasn't just about a bunny and some hens.

Nope, it was about an even greater loss. I hadn't really cried when my mother died. I had been so brave and practical then. The whole family had been. If one of us had started to cry, then the rest of us would have lost it. We are not weepers in my family. We are "stiff upper lip" Episcopalians. At the funeral, my mother's minister, the man who had officiated at my wedding, too, said her death, and every death, should "shake" us into a new way of thinking and being. I had been thinking about that for about a year. Had I just transferred all my anger and pain about my mother's death, and I suppose also about my accident, to that poor family that already had their hands full without a crazy woman next door? Which is not to say that they shouldn't deal with that bad dog, but *is* to say that I may have overreacted just a tad.

A few days later I walked over and apologized to them. I shouldn't have behaved that way, especially in front of the children. It was a short encounter and we did not become friends. I said the right words, but my heart had not noticeably shifted.

A MONTH LATER I was doing spring yard work between squalls, when a goshawk flew low toward the chicken coop, looking for an easy meal. The fenced-in chicken run is open at the top. I raised my rake and ran to protect them, like a good Mr. McGregor, but the surviving hens had already beat it up the ramp into the chicken-sized door of their sturdy coop.

Chip says that what chickens lack in brains they make up for with instinct. Maybe what humans lack in understanding we make up for with faith. I do know deep down that there is something good about this world — and that something is love. You don't have to be a Christian to know that's why we keep picking each other up every time we fall down. You just have to be human. I hope that someday I'll really love my neighbors, especially the difficult ones, half as much as I love my chickens and half as much as Mark loved total strangers on the other side of the world. In the meantime, I'll keep going to my church, because I know what our vicar, Jan, would say about this. It's the same message she preached on "Love Your Neighbor Sunday," and the same one she reiterates in one form or another every Sunday. We are called by Jesus to be good to all people, even those we don't think we like, much less love, and even those bad dogs among us. This, and only this, will ever shake up the world enough to change it.

CHAPTER **9**

The Comfort of Eagles

And he will raise you up
on eagle's wings.
— "Eagle's Wings," a gospel hymn

I was driving back from town to our house when I came
upon a dozen bald eagles calling, swooping, and coasting over the road between the tall spruce trees and the
river delta. The silver salmon were spawning, and their
carcasses littered the beach. The eagles were there for the
free lunch. One flew so close to the windshield I could see
individual feathers on its wings. The shadow it cast on my
Subaru station wagon reached from bumper to bumper.
A full-grown eagle's wings span seven feet; they are the
biggest backyard birds you'll ever see.

Even though there was a roof over my head, I ducked.
A second later an eyeless fish head dropped from the sky
to the pavement, and two more eagles jumped on it, right
next to my car door. I stopped and rolled down the window

to get a better look. For a heartbeat I wondered if being this close to a couple of eagles was dangerous, but before I could decide it was, one of them grabbed the salmon head in its talons and took off, with the other in pursuit, gliding and flapping over the lush beach grass, the wild roses, and on up the broad river valley. This is what Emerson must have had in mind when he wrote that "the proper response to the world is applause."

Betty Holgate was out on her ride-on lawn mower so I pulled into her circular drive to say hello and marvel at my eagle encounter. Betty and Don have the biggest lawn on our road. I'm pretty sure it's the biggest lawn in Haines, which is not really a lawn kind of place. Most of the brambly yards on Betty's side of Mud Bay Road lost ground when the state upgraded it from gravel to pavement. The Holgates' property was scheduled to be cut in half until they informed the engineers that the tall spruce way down at the corner where their driveway meets the road was an eagle nesting tree. The state swung the new road around the tree, and the Holgates kept their big yard. Such is the power of eagles.

As I drove up, Betty pulled over, shut off her mower, and hollered, "Did you see the show?" I didn't have to ask if she meant the eagles. Even though everyone around here knows that eagles are opportunistic scavengers and that where there's free food, you'll find them, we still admire them. You can't help it. They demand your attention.

A little like our friend John Katzeek. He thinks nothing of calling at seven on a weekday morning, asking, "What's for breakfast?" and, before I can even answer, adding, "I'm coming over; put the coffee on." John drinks only decaf, so we keep his beans in a separate jar. John is a Tlingit clan leader or, more accurately, the keeper of Klukwan's Tall Fin Killer Whale House (*Keet Gooshi Hit* in Tlingit). He is also part of the Eagle moiety. As I said when I told you about Wayne's totem pole, I am no expert on Tlingit culture, so forgive me if I err. I do know that Tlingits are members of either the Eagle or Raven moiety and that those main cultural trunks are divided into many branches of other clans and houses that people are affiliated with. Some of the houses, like John's, actually exist and hold the clan regalia, carvings, and objects that tell its history. Those houses and their contents are used on ceremonial occasions, mostly having to do with death — from wakes to the more elaborate potlatches held about a year after a funeral. Other houses are gone now, but their names and family associations remain, as well as some of the regalia, which is stored elsewhere. John has called Haines and the nearby Tlingit village of Klukwan home all his life. His ancestors have lived in the Chilkat Valley since the last ice age.

I know John because he and Chip hunt together. They have become friends slowly, in the way grown men from different backgrounds rarely do. While John is as local as the weather, my husband is a newcomer. Of colonial New England and immigrant Norwegian Minnesota farmer stock, Chip has lived in John's territory for only about twenty-five years. John has brown skin and black hair with a shock of gray up front. He graduated from Haines High School and earns a living as a hunting guide. My husband is tall, fair, and balding and has a master's degree in forestry and environmental studies from Yale, but of the two of them, John is the expert on Alaskan natural history. It's safe to say John is teaching us all a lot.

John's father, Tom Katzeek, known as Tom Kat, raised his sons in a traditional Tlingit way, surrounded by grandparents, aunts, uncles, and cousins in Klukwan and Haines. "Every night my grandfather would have the same talk after dinner—and every dinner was a kind of Thanksgiving," John tells me. "For an hour or more, it was always the same stories: who we were and where we came from." John and his five brothers were with his Klukwan grandparents frequently because Tom Kat and John's mother, Isabell, were working at the cannery on Mud Bay Road, the old red one down past my house, packing salmon into cans. The myths and legends John heard at the village dinner table were more than entertainment. On the one hand John is completely modern; he is definitely not the crying Indian of those old anti-pollution campaigns. His hair is trimmed short, he smells of aftershave, and he wears creased flannel shirts, cleaner blue jeans than Chip, and good leather hiking boots. On the other hand he is very much a traditional Tlingit. He believes the historical and spiritual truths in the old stories. For instance, about thirty years ago John's father was out on the Chilkat River when an otter appeared and told Tom Kat his oldest son would die. Tom Kat knew the legends about otters bearing bad news and understood that the only way to prevent the otter's prediction from coming true was to kill it. A few days later John learned that he had potentially terminal cancer. John is alive today, he says, because his father killed that otter.

WHEN JOHN ARRIVED for breakfast one morning, I told him I was working on an essay about eagles for an Alaskan wildlife anthology and asked him what I should write. He answered the way I knew he would. "Tell them you are married to one."

It's true. John adopted Chip at a big party last October where the Eagles and the Ravens gathered to honor a deceased elder. When an Eagle or a Raven dies, the other clan supports them in their immediate grief at the time of the funeral. Then after a year or two, the moiety on the receiving end pays the members of the other one back, thanking them with food, music, dance, money, and many gifts in what is usually called a potlatch, or pay-off party. The proper Tlingit term, though, is *Khoo.éex'*, which means to call, or invite. The *Khoo.éex'* also ends the mourning period. At these events, new members may be adopted into the tribe and, in this way, when someone dies a few more folks are added. Tlingits adopt friends or individuals who support the culture, but not in the way babies are adopted, or even the way my daughter Stoli was adopted by us. Being adopted into a Tlingit family is to be adopted into a way of life. You don't move in together; you probably don't even share Thanksgiving dinner. It's not that kind of relationship. If you are adopted by Tlingit friends, you support the traditions and the values and especially, as they say, you "show your face" by attending Tlingit community events.

After breakfast, John asked if I wanted to ride up the river with him in his airboat, to see if the bears were moving out of their winter dens yet or if the trumpeter swans were back. He keeps his boats in Klukwan. We lurched down the potholed village road by the school, down between one-story ranch-style homes with pastel vinyl siding, decks facing the river, and wood smoke drifting from metal chimney pipes. We made our way slowly—the village speed limit is 15 mph—past rusted rigs, skiffs on trailers, four-wheelers, snow machines, satellite TV dishes, and loose dogs. Aside from the new traditionally designed hand-hewn post and timber tribal house, my favorite buildings are the derelict turn-of-the-century Bureau of Indian Affairs structures. They were built in the Greek revival style and have no paint left on them at all—the Chilkat River dust has sanded the cedar a steel gray, from dentil moldings to clapboards. Some are roofless; others lean far to the right or left. Still others are upright and hollow-eyed, with no glass in the windows. The former government school, though, has been restored and painted white, and it retains its functional beauty as the Chilkat Indian Village office. In front, there's a community garden, and nearby is the veterans memorial park, with a monument, flag poles, and two warrior totem poles.

If you don't step out of the truck in Klukwan, if you aren't invited to see a riverbank smokehouse or the young men carving a totem pole down by the new traditional knowledge camp, if you have never been to a funeral in the Alaska Native Sisterhood Hall or to one of the many after-death ritual feasts, you might think Klukwan is kind of shabby, especially in springtime, when the melting snow reveals piles of junk and general disarray. (Haines doesn't look much better at this time of year; when my father visits each summer he grumbles that no one seems to care about their yards. "Haven't you people ever heard of a weed whacker?" he'll say. One trip he even painted the trim on our lumberyard because he couldn't stand to see the paint peeling.) Also, if you aren't invited to spend some time in Klukwan, you may never know how peaceful and productive some of its households are or just how much the rhythm of life in the village is tied to the seasons and what's for dinner tonight and what will be for dinner two months from tonight.

In addition to guiding big-game hunters, John, along with his wife, Cheryl, offers a paid tour of the Tall Fin Killer Whale House in Klukwan. The tour includes a look inside his tribal house, and sometimes there is traditional dancing and singing by the student dance troupe from the Klukwan School. But like a first impression of the village, Tlingit song and dance taken out of context reveals only part of the story. It's the difference between singing a few Christmas carols at a party and singing hymns at a candlelight mass on Christmas Eve. It's the difference between eating crackers and drinking wine and taking Communion.

My friend Kimberley Strong, the Klukwan Village Council president, has a hard time leaving her riverfront home to drive to town in the summertime when there is so much to do. Kimberley has worked as a law clerk and, like John, served on the board of one of the region's largest corporations, Klukwan, Inc., a logging, construction, and tourism–based corporation owned by the village. It was once a multimillion-dollar operation but has fallen on hard times. She's also on the school board, the electricity co-op board, and the Chilkat Valley Community Foundation Board, and is a leader in the Alaska Native Sisterhood, a civil rights and social organization. "I'm basically a professional volunteer," she acknowledges, and if you ask her how she supports herself, Kimberley will tell you with *subsistence,* the Alaskan word for living off the land.

When she smokes her fish, Kimberley faces the split carcasses upstream for the first half of the drying and then turns them on the greased smokehouse poles and heads them downstream for the final smoke, just like John does—it's so their spirits will return to the sea to guide next year's salmon back up the river again. The black soil in the community garden Kimberley helps tend produces basketball-sized cabbages, sweet carrots, peas, squash, and greens of all kinds. Klukwan's fingerling potatoes come from stock hundreds of years old. The steep mountain foothills that rise behind the village are covered with blueberry bushes; there are nets extending out in the river from nearly every backyard, and smokehouses are in continuous use from June to September. In the spring, eulachon (pronounced "hooligan"), a smelt prized for its oil—"Omega threes," John tells me, "good for your cholesterol"—are caught in dip nets, fermented in pits, and then boiled in vats to release the oil that is skimmed off and put in jars to be used later for dressing salmon or seal meat or to stir into cranberries and salmon eggs. In the fall, moose are hunted, butchered, canned, and frozen. This year Kimberley and her women-only hunting party had more success than John and Chip did in the annual moose hunt, shooting a big bull in the first hours.

John stopped the truck in the muddy lot next to his smokehouse. There's a locked chain-link gate on his long open shed. Inside are several boats and motors and a fuel tank and hose. He filled up two plastic gas jugs and grabbed a quart of oil, and we headed out of the village and toward his other boat landing farther upstream. "Too much dust," he explained. "I can't leave the airboat here until the water is higher; the dust ruins the engine." In the early spring, the river is low. The snows haven't melted up high yet, so water flows in meandering channels through the gravel, sand, and fine gray chalk-like dust of the wide, wide valley. On your bare feet, on a warm July day, it could be the same soft sand of a well-groomed pitcher's mound. When John and Kimberley's ancestors first settled in Klukwan, about six thousand years ago (there is also some evidence that humans lived in the region as far back as ten thousand years ago), geologists theorize that the village was at the head of a twenty-mile-long fjord. The Tlingits sailed up it in deep dugout canoes from the beach in front of my house. In the centuries since then, the glacial-sediment-bearing river has dropped one thousand feet of natural fill into that underwater canyon.

An alluvial fan, where the Chilkat is joined by two other rivers, lets water percolate through the sand and gravel all summer, creating an underground reservoir that bubbles back up in the winter. It keeps the river ice-free from November to February and thus attracts the largest concentration of bald eagles in the world. Some three thousand gather near the village each autumn to feast on the carcasses of spawning salmon in the only open water for miles. The eagles have come here since "time immemorial," as the Tlingits say, because of the warm upwellings and for the easy meals those rotting spawned-out salmon provide.

Every November, Haines hosts an eagle festival, with guided eagle viewings and special programs for photographers, artists, and naturalists. The highlight is the release of rehabilitated injured eagles back into the Chilkat Bald Eagle Preserve, forty thousand acres of critical eagle habitat adjacent to Klukwan. The American Bald Eagle Foundation organizes the event and ties this flight into patriotism, since the eagle is our national symbol. They call it the Flight to Freedom. In that great American way, the privilege of releasing a bird is auctioned off to the highest bidder to raise money for the foundation and the festival and to rehabilitate more eagles. The eagles are transported to the preserve from town in large dog kennels, which are carried out to the center of a circle of spectators and participants on the riverbank. It's usually snowy and often bitterly cold, and it takes a while for all the speeches, the photographs, and the auction. The last time I went, a woman had bid eight hundred dollars for this opportunity, and she wanted to hold the eagle as she set it free. The handler wore talon-proof gloves and helped her sort of half-hold the raptor, which was wrapped tightly in a blanket. She wanted to kiss the eagle, as well, but that was way too dangerous. An eagle's beak is razor sharp. She was so overcome by the experience that she wept. Eagles can make people who aren't used to them very emotional.

They can make people who are used to them emotional, too. I stood there, looking at the birding world's paparazzi, the local dignitaries, the sponsors' banners flapping, and that woman sobbing and clutching her breast, and part of me thought it was all way over the top. But here's the thing:

even though I have seen hundreds of wet eagles hunched in the cottonwoods along the river on rainy fall days with their white heads tucked into the shoulders of their ruffled brown coats, like old men in a city park—grumpy eagles that look more like Walter Matthau than an ad for the Air Force—even though that's where my mind was, when that woman half-tossed, half-dropped that eagle into the air and he glided away from us without even a tip of his wing, he took a part of me with him. I made a good wish, the same way I do on the first evening star.

As the public eagle releases during the festival grew in size and popularity, the people of Klukwan asked the festival organizers if they could hold a private ceremony. There are no microphones, no fences, and no auctions at that one. It's down by a log smokehouse at the edge of the village on the riverbank a few feet from the water. There is Native singing, dancing, and prayers for eagles, salmon, and the people whose lives and spirits are so closely intertwined with them.

Villagers wear their ceremonial best: the carved wooden clan hats; the red and blue button-trimmed blankets; the black, white, and yellow Chilkat blankets; woven headbands; and beaded moose-hide slippers. This year the elders chose a young woman who teaches Tlingit at the village school to release the eagle. She quietly opened the kennel door and the bird stepped out. It would be nice to tell you that this eagle responded to the more reverent setting differently than her brother had at the bigger release.

It would be nice to report that she had looked her Tlingit relatives in the eyes and made a spiritual connection. But that's not what happened. She took off so fast and so fiercely that the little children in the front row ducked and the cameras missed it entirely. It is always tricky, and often disappointing, to attribute to animals traits we'd want to see in humans.

Many people know that Ben Franklin objected to the bald eagle as the choice for our national symbol because of its behavior. "He is a bird of bad moral character," Franklin wrote. A cynic, observing American politics today, might say that our forefathers knew exactly what they were doing. In the days before Alaskan statehood, fox farmers said eagles stole their cubs, and fishermen said they ate their salmon, so a bounty was put on them. From 1917 to 1953, hunters were paid anywhere from $0.50 to $2.50 per dead eagle. More than one hundred thousand were legally shot dead, and many more deaths were never reported. "That's how we got grocery money in lean winters," one old-timer told me.

Sometimes we tell tourists stories about eagles. We all like the one about the dachshund in Sitka that was picked up during a backyard picnic by an eagle and then dropped a few yards later because he was too heavy. But even jaded Alaskans can see there is much in the eagle's character to respect. They mate for life; they build sturdy homes, returning to them year after year; and they take good care of their babies, most of the time. I have read that more than half of all young eagles do not survive their first flight, but I don't believe it. I have never come upon a dead fledgling at the bottom of a nesting tree and don't know anyone who has. Betty, a pilot, watches the young eagles launch out of the nest in her front yard each spring. Once, she told me, one almost crashed to the ground, but at the last minute he pulled up and soared off. "He must not have had a very good flight instructor," she said, "but he figured it out."

Eagles often watch me from the treetops, their white heads bright against the dark spruce branches, when I garden. I imagine that they enjoy my company. They have never shown any interest at all in kidnapping my terrier, Phoebe, but then again, Phoebe is fairly feisty and not meaty enough to be worth the effort catching her would require. Even though there are rumors each fall of eagles killing cats, I have seen an eagle eat only one, and I'm pretty sure it was already dead—it had been hit by a car—when the eagle pulled it off the macadam and flew off with it.

If you go out on the river flats near the village of Kluk-wan with John, under a gibbous December moon, and skid a canoe over the blue-white snow, slip it into the black mirrored water, and paddle across to the line of bare cottonwoods etched against the white mountains, you will be surprised that it is not a silent night at all. You will see and hear hundreds of calling and cackling eagles, dragging salmon out of the river, fighting over them, and tearing them apart with their talons and beaks. Those who want eagles to sound courageous or at least as distinguished as hawks are usually let down. Eagles have a high singsongy kind of whistle when they call from trees, roofs, or telephone poles. They chatter like seagulls. As much as I'd love them to, they don't speak English.

But they may speak Tlingit.

I suspect there is some telepathy when it comes to birds and animals and the Tlingit people. When John and I finally had his airboat going—it's one of those flat-bottomed skiffs with an airplane propeller on the back that you see in films about the Everglades, only smaller and homemade—it was so loud we had to put on headphones. I was more than a little disheartened. John had promised we'd see wildlife: swans, moose, bears, eagles, and "maybe some wolves." Surely this roaring plane of a boat would scare off every creature for miles. But as we floated swiftly up the river, in that oddly quiet headphoned world, the swans gliding in the sloughs turned to look but stayed put. The eagles didn't leave their cottonwood perches. Later, on a sandbar where we'd stopped for lunch, I asked John about that. He said the birds and animals were used to his boat, as they had been back when his father, Tom Kat, had a similar one. He said they could recognize a friend. Do I believe this? It may sound crazy, but I think I might. I don't have a better explanation.

. . .

JOHN AND CHIP HAD become clan brothers at a big *Khoo.éex'* party for a couple hundred guests at the Klukwan Alaska Native Sisterhood Hall that featured more food and gifts in one place than I had ever seen. These are not rich people. But since everything in Tlingit society is reciprocal, John says it is important to be as generous as you are able, because the next time you may be on the receiving end. There's more to this deep giving, this distribution of wealth, than I'll ever know, but that's the simplest way to explain it. This memorial party for Austin Brown, a Tlingit leader from Juneau with Klukwan connections who had died two years previously, reminded me of Thanksgiving, Christmas, and Easter all in one. The Eagle hosts gave gifts to their Raven guests all day and all night. There were so many that the Eagles walked up and down the aisles between the dining tables in teams, with one holding a box of socks and jam or canned goods, and another distributing them.

By the time I was handed a new thermal blanket, I was out of room for any more presents on my lap, the table, and the floor. I already had a grocery bag full of fruit and boxes filled with cans of Vienna sausages, pork and beans, fruit cocktail, and corn. There were new socks, jars of thimbleberry and salmonberry jam, soap, coffee beans, microwave popcorn, pens, oven mitts, half-pints of smoked salmon, and lots of Top Ramen.

"It wouldn't be a potlatch without Top Ramen," noted my friend Tony Tengs, one of the dozen or so non-Natives in the crowded hall. He was with his mother, Helen, and nephew, Marty; they had all been adopted a long time ago. Everyone rose, shaking the ramen packages and doing a sort of Tlingit jig to the rhythmic chanting. I was glad for the activity. I was sleepy and very full. It was after midnight, and more than twelve hours had passed since the event began. I had eaten pilot bread; smoked salmon spread; berries; moose stew with biscuits; herring roe salad; salmon and rice; prime rib with potatoes, gravy, and carrots; and, most recently, fishy Tlingit-style lox with cream cheese on a toasted bagel. When he invited us, John warned that the one thing that must never be said at a potlatch is "No, thank you," and that it's important to eat whatever's on your plate. So I ate the sweet-and-sour seal, the fry bread with honey, the salmon eggs preserved in eulachon oil. Like the other guests, I had left my seat only during the handful of designated breaks in the singing and dancing and feasting. In the daylight I'd used that time to walk around the village and look up at the red, gold, and green mountainsides colored like an oriental rug and frosted on top with the first snow, which reminded me of powdered sugar. (Must be all that food going to my head.) But after dark, when the bears were out, I stayed closer to the back porch of the hall. The fresh air felt good, and I listened to the river and the ravens and eagles calling and singing in the trees.

John is an Eagle, and since he was doing the adopting, Chip would be an Eagle. I hadn't seen much of Chip at the potlatch; he couldn't even sit with me. He helped his fellow Eagles cook, serve, and distribute piles of gifts. The Eagle hosts wouldn't sit down at all at this party—they even ate standing up. Although I had no official status, John instructed me to join the Ravens at the long butcher-papered tables. This was what was meant by the reciprocity I mentioned earlier. Ravens and Eagles represent the two sides of the Tlingit society and fit together to make a whole, similar to the Asian concept of yin and yang. An Eagle elder may not speak to a community gathering unless a Raven elder says a few words, too. They say it throws them off balance otherwise.

Memorial potlatches are held in the fall because that's when there is the most food to share and when the summer gathering and fishing are done. Just as at our house, it's the season when smoked salmon and jam are in jars, and fish and game are in the freezer. The apples have been made into pies and the last carrots have been pulled. It is also still relatively easy to travel, since the winter storms haven't yet begun. In this way, the gathering of the Tlingit people is similar to the natural congregation of wild eagles with which this party happened to coincide. The human Eagles and Ravens there that night came from all over southeast Alaska and the Yukon Territory.

Our Eagle hosts not only cooked all the food and distributed gifts, they also entertained us. They told lots of jokes, some in Tlingit, most in English. They sang pop tunes karaoke style, jazz standards, and ancient Tlingit songs. Tony stood and sassily crooned "I Am My Own Grandpa," which everyone loved because Tlingits often really are their own grandparents. A baby named for a grandfather is sometimes called "Grandpa" and when, as an adult, he is asked to say a few words at a *Khoo.éex'* like this, he will preface the most important parts with, "I am my grandfather speaking now." One elderly Juneau woman whom I had pegged as a stern keeper-of-tradition type—she has steel-gray hair and teaches Tlingit language classes at the University of Alaska Southeast—proved me wrong when she and her equally serious-looking family presented their well-rehearsed "Mrs. Don Ho" musical review. It featured Hawaiian costumes, the singing of "Tiny Bubbles" in Tlingit, and hula dancing. John surprised me even more, joining them in the act, wearing a blue clown wig and, later, his clan regalia and dancing and singing with his Tall Fin Killer Whale brothers and sisters. There was so much more—some slapstick, some solemn, some I understood, much I didn't, and all the while more gifts were given and more food was served at the long tables under the bright lights of the full community hall.

I could write a whole book about what happened to a Chilkat blanket created by master weaver Anna Brown Ehlers of Juneau. After formally presenting it as a gift, she announced she would cut it in pieces. There was a long silence as the heavy king-sized, shawl-shaped blanket was lifted down from the wall it had been displayed on and draped over a table. The room remained quiet as Anna carefully cut it up into about twenty small sections, a foot or so square, that she gave away to some of the Eagles, including John, whose piece had a killer whale pattern on it.

The blanket, woven in the traditional way from mountain goat wool, was worth many thousands of dollars. The ancient and modern weavers from Klukwan are famous for their skill at creating distinctive fringed white, blue, yellow, and black dancing blankets. The first time I saw one was in New York's American Museum of Natural History, on a field trip as a child. The museum's main hall, lined with totem poles, held a huge Chilkat Tlingit war canoe with a dozen life-sized mannequins in it, all draped in the now-familiar blankets. They take years to make and there are only a handful of true master weavers like Anna alive today. That's why there was silence when she said she would destroy her work in order to repair a tear in the fabric of the tribe that had happened so long ago that most people in the room, Native and non-Native, didn't even know the details. Anna's father, Austin Brown, had known, though, and it was his dying wish that she do this to make whatever went wrong right again. Anna smiled as she cut that blanket and gave the sections away.

After that, the adoption ceremony was fairly anticlimactic. The names of the half-dozen new clan members were called in English. One at a time they walked up to the front of the hall where an elder pressed a twenty-dollar bill on their forehead (it can be any denomination—a five or ten will do just as well). Each was given a Tlingit name, which was then repeated by the crowd several times. The bill was handed to the clan member responsible for remembering the adoptee's new name and reminding them of their duties to the tribe. When I asked what that was all about, three Tlingit friends could not tell me, except to say it's tradition; in that way, they reminded me of Tevye's song from *Fiddler on the Roof.* I'm pretty sure I've explained this all correctly, but I'm certain I've missed some cultural subtleties. I was so full and so groggy I was nodding off. Tlingit protocol could take a lifetime to learn. Even the names can be challenging. The ceremony happened so quickly and it was so late that it took Chip a couple of days to figure out what his Tlingit name actually was. Now we sometimes call him *Keet-woo-saa-nee,* or *Keet* for short (we are still not sure how to spell the rest of it), especially when he's hanging around with John.

It was almost five in the morning when we finally made our way out of the thick air of the hall and into the cool of the predawn darkness. As Chip and I walked toward our truck on the frosted road, I listened with new ears to the rhythm of the wind in the cottonwoods, the steady backbeat of the river, the voices of the people who have accompanied them for as long as time, and wondered how to properly thank John and his clan. My own tradition of a written thank-you note seemed too small. Then I remembered what an Eagle elder had expressed hours earlier, the day before actually. David Katzeek, a blood relative of John's, had said, "If you just say 'thank you' that is a great speech. Sometimes thank you is the greatest speech you can make." He also stressed that it is better to use the Tlingit word for thank you than the English one, even if you mispronounce it.

"*Gunalcheesh,*" I said softly to all the eagles, both human and animal, who I couldn't see but knew were out there in the dark. "*Gunalcheesh,*" I whispered again, practicing the unfamiliar lift of my tongue on the back of my palate. "*Gunalcheesh,*" I called out one more time, before I fell asleep in the front seat of Chip's truck as it rocked gently down the village road toward home.

CHAPTER 10

Snowshoeing with God: A Playlist

And if I am to do nothing, let me do it gallantly.
—Book of Common Prayer

I n Shin Buddhism there is a type of prayer or meditation called deep hearing, which is sometimes translated
as "hearing the light." This, some practitioners believe,
comes when you use your body to pay attention; when
you walk you *attend* to the walking itself. In Alaska, with
a solid six months of winter, walking in quiet places often
requires snowshoes. I snowshoe with Chip some days, but
many days, I choose to go alone, sort of. My dogs, Forte,
a bouncy flat-coated retriever; Merry, a gentle fifteen-
year-old gray-faced lab-husky mix; and Phoebe, a scrappy
terrier who sports a red jacket, come, too.

When I snowshoe with the dogs I don't hear the light
so much as I do Merle Haggard. And, no, I don't have an
iPod. The music that accompanies me on these treks is in
my head; the walking simply brings it forth. I don't know

all the words to all the songs that bubble up and out of me as I walk — the ones I hear and then give voice to — so I'll hum and make up a line or two. It seems to me that marching along in the woods singing is doing nothing about as gallantly as a person can, as the Episcopal healing prayer says. Hiking is good for the legs, and singing is good for the heart. When you combine the two, at the very least you'll be prepared to audition for *The Sound of Music,* although I sing from *Oklahoma!* more often, especially the song about corn growing "as high as an elephant's eye." I like *Guys and Dolls,* too ("Luck Be a Lady" and "If I Were a Bell"), and *Fiddler on the Roof* ("Miracle of Miracles" and "Do You Love Me?"). I do love to sing "Centerfield" by John Fogerty. "Put me in coach, I'm ready to play," I'll shout coming around the bend before Moose Meadow, and when I do, I believe I just may play shortstop again for my old softball team, the Diehards.

I snowshoe that way, sometimes for an hour and a half, sometimes for three or four or even five hours, if I go all the way up to the summit. It's not as though I plan to sing. I begin my walk thinking and, I suppose in a way, praying, in those informal conversations with God that sometimes feel more as if you are talking to yourself but that usually manage to help make challenges more manageable and less scary. Once I let the worries off my chest, the humming starts, and soon I'm singing out loud.

In *Dakota*, Kathleen Norris writes that one of the more surprising aspects of monastic life is how frequently monks sing as they attend to chores and their prayers. Singing, she notes, is both play and worship. Sometimes I sing country-western favorites, the ones I play when I volunteer at the radio station, romantic tunes like Jimmy Buffett's "Come Monday" and Lefty Frizzell's "That's the Way Love Goes" (Merle Haggard made it a hit). He sings about throwing horseshoes over his left shoulder, searching for four-leaf clovers, and love, the kind of love that is always right there with you. "That's the music God made," I half-hum. "It's never old." Seeking God's mercy is a lot like wishing for good luck—both require faith that such a thing is possible. Emmylou Harris had it right when she equated a rosary with a rabbit's foot in another favorite tune of mine, "Love and Happiness," which is also on what I like to think of as my "snowshoeing with God" playlist.

I always feel better after singing Lyle Lovett's "God Will," in which he asks an old girlfriend: Who will forgive your lying and cheating? And then answers, "God will, but I won't, and that's the difference between God and me."

Once—and I hope you don't think I'm completely crazy for sharing this—standing under a really big spruce tree, one that would take three or four people with linked arms to circle, a tree that I had never even noticed before I was slowed by injuries, I burst into the doxology "Praise God from whom all blessings flow." It practically sang itself. On sleepier mornings, when I don't climb as high, I often pause at a knob overlooking the valley below and sing a verse of an old spiritual that Nancy Nash plays after Communion in church, "When I fall on my knees with my face to the rising sun / O Lord, have mercy on me." The way I feel doing that helps me understand why Muslims are moved to drop to their knees facing Mecca five times a day. And no matter what month it is, if snow is falling, I nearly always sing "Winter Wonderland" somewhere along the trail. It can't be helped.

One afternoon I went snowshoeing later than usual. There was a lot on my mind. I had written four obituaries in a week, and talking with the families had been hard. It wasn't the first time since my accident that I felt guilty for being alive when other, very good people hadn't been as lucky. I decided to climb for an hour and a half and then head back downhill in the long nautical twilight of Alaska's winter nights. That day, with so much on my mind, I sang more softly, Leonard Cohen's "Hallelujah" and the Beatles' "I Will." I snowshoed as mindfully as I ever have, tuned to the swish of my footsteps, my steady breath, the snow dropping off a bough, the gray tree trunks, the white ground, and the violet sky. The low sun slanted through the forest in long stripes; there was no wind at all, and it was as silent as snow. The air had a wispy shimmer I'd never seen before. I stepped off the trail and shuffled through the knee-high powder toward a knoll to get a better view of the inlet below, while my dogs watched me curiously. I stood there, doing nothing, for a long moment.

God was near, and I listened for His light.

CHAPTER 11

Passing the Peace

The peace of the Lord
be always with you.
—Book of Common Prayer

In our church every Sunday we "pass the peace." We turn to our neighbors, shake hands, and say, "The peace of the Lord be always with you," and they respond, "And also with you." Or at least that's how we are supposed to do it, according to the Book of Common Prayer. We usually just say, "Lord's peace" or plain "Peace." Since there are only about a dozen of us, we walk around and greet each person. Sometimes there are hugs and often quiet conversations about why we need a little peace, or about our gratitude for receiving it.

Episcopalians do this seventh-inning stretch with a purpose. It comes over halfway through the service, after the lessons, prayers, and what I like to think of as "the business" end of Sunday worship, before the more serious, introspective, and spiritual conclusion: Communion, or Holy Eucharist. The weekly reminder of Christ's death and resurrection is heavy stuff, even for those of us who reenact it regularly. The break for peace happens right after the confession of sin. That's when we acknowledge having not loved our neighbors as ourselves and not loving God with our whole hearts. We ask forgiveness, out loud and in unison, for what we have done and "left undone." Trust me, the silent inner itemized list is long and it is why, in large part, I attend church. It's why I practice my religion. It's also why, when Father Bob Morin, a Catholic priest, said, "Church is not a bunker, it is a diving board to the world," I knew exactly what he meant. Then he quoted Søren Kierkegaard, "Jesus does not need admirers; he needs followers."

In other words, following the teachings of Jesus has very little to do with kneeling before His cross and everything to do with standing up for the things He did. The trick is knowing if what you are standing up for is what Jesus meant. That whole "What would Jesus do?" question is a lot less simple than you'd think. It is, as Father Bob says, a question that can only be answered by listening to what God is saying, rather than putting words in His mouth. Or as C. S. Lewis famously observed, he didn't pray in order for God to understand him, rather so he would understand God. Obviously, I'm not the first person to ponder this.

When Dr. Martin Luther King Jr. was at a low point

during his struggle for civil rights, he confessed that he was afraid he was losing his courage, and if people saw him do that, they'd lose theirs. He asked God if it was better to pray for change or to march for change, and he said—and this is what I think truly separates holy men and women from the rest of us—God answered him. God told Dr. King to get off his knees and stand up for righteousness, truth, and justice.

On the other hand, I had been asking God for a week what to do about a peace march planned to protest the ongoing war in Iraq. Is it better to walk through town for peace or stay at home and pray about it? I had not received an answer. God did not call back. He did not wake me in the middle of night with a shout or even whisper to me during a snowshoe in the woods.

But I hadn't given up. I had been attending a Lenten retreat with Father Bob at the Sacred Heart Catholic Church every night for a week. He traveled to Haines from Minnesota to give a lecture series to the parish and those similarly sentimented, like me. There were about ten of us. The weather may have had something to do with the small turnout; it snowed hard every time we met. Anyway, Father Bob spoke with as much animation, preparation, and assumption of a certain level of education and worldliness as if he were in a packed university lecture hall. He's from Boston originally, and a member of the Missionary Oblates of Mary Immaculate. Founded by a Frenchman in 1816, the Oblates accentuate the positive in order to help people find the good within themselves. They travel the world preaching the gospel. Father Bob lectures all over the country, and not just in big places but in small, out-of-the-way communities like Haines. The early Oblates did not condemn so-called sinners who went to the bars instead of attending mass; instead, they met them in the taverns and befriended and helped them. As Father Bob said, "Anyone can tell you what's wrong with you—we tell you what's right."

THERE WAS A LOT right about Jim Phair, a furnace and heating system repairman from New York who had never lost his thick accent, had a friendly way about him, and sported a droopy old-fashioned mustache. The first time we met, Jim said, "I've heard you're from New York, too, aren't you?" and wondered why I didn't sound like it. My New York was more suburban and, I suspect, more affluent than his. But here's the thing about Jim: When I was around him, I wished I had a real New York accent, too. I wished my voice sounded more Brooklyn and less NPR. When I was around Jim I wanted to be more like him. I wanted to be his friend. I think everybody did.

Jim maintained the funky heating systems in the Chilkat Center for the Arts, the former cannery building turned theater where we have church on Sundays, and which Lee Heinmiller, who lives across the alley, has also kept watch over for many years. It was not uncommon to see the bearded and ponytailed Lee, limping on bad knees that have bowed from years of Tlingit dancing with the now-defunct Chilkat Indian Dancers, and big Jim, with his Vietnam veteran's cap and Army camouflage jacket, banging on pipes before church on cold Sunday mornings. Jim didn't mind being called out on weekends or nights. He liked to help and he liked talking with you while he worked. It was almost as common to see Jim's truck parked in a pullout along the river just past the airport when Chip and I were riding our bikes at five on summer mornings. He'd be there sleeping off a hard night or perhaps continuing one. When Jim was drinking, it was difficult to be around him. I suppose he knew that and removed himself from the community.

When Jim's liver failed, he was so ill that his wife put him into a veterans' home in Stony Brook, New York, out on Long Island, and she and their daughter moved back east to be closer to him and the rest of their family. Six months later he died. I was writing the obituary and contacted the family on the phone and via email, but the pain from the loss was still too distracting for them, and they asked me to wait until they were more prepared to share Jim's story. While time may not heal, it does give you perspective.

Considering how Jim had died, the way he had abruptly left Haines, and the sorrow his passing had brought to his family, it was a surprise when, three months later, a tribute to Jim, written by his wife, Joanne, was read at her request at the annual Veterans Day dinner at the Haines American Legion. It was brave and frank and a reminder that not all casualties of war take place on the battlefield. "His battle with alcohol was his undoing," Joanne wrote. "The years of abuse took their toll. Despite Herculean efforts by the best EMT staff any town could ask for, extensive help at the clinic and the VA, Jim's condition deteriorated to the point where he spent five months at Juneau's Bartlett Hospital before being transported to the Long Island Veterans Home."

It was a long way from the Alaskan dream that had brought the Phairs here in 1989, a lifelong desire of Jim's spurred on by stories of his grandfather's Klondike gold field adventures and subsequent years spent prospecting in the Wrangell–St. Elias Mountains, where he had owned the North Midas Copper Company. Jim proudly took over Haines Heating Service on Alaska Day, in 1993, which he took to be a very good sign. I began working on his obituary by rereading the tribute at the Legion and then I called and emailed Joanne, who had remained in New York, for the rest of the information, which this time she willingly gave. Because of the circumstances of Jim's death, I decided to let Joanne tell much of his life story, and I quoted her extensively. It was a departure from the way I usually write obituaries; in our paper they are news pieces, rather than the paid commentaries submitted by family members that most papers publish on the obituary page. I also did it because, since my own trauma, I realized how much sharing the details had helped me to heal.

James Joseph Phair III was born in 1950 and grew up on Long Island. As a teenager he had learned his trade in a steamfitter's apprenticeship program. He left high school a month after turning seventeen to voluntarily serve in Vietnam. "Jim was very proud of the fact that the Phairs had fought in every war since the Civil War and always considered himself a soldier by birth," Joanne wrote. He learned to drive tanks in Germany and arrived in Vietnam in time for the Tet Offensive. Joanne noted that he saw "extensive combat for nine months," until his camp was bombed and he suffered severe injuries to his leg and chest, was sent home, honorably discharged, and issued a Purple Heart in 1970. But he "had a very difficult time upon his return to a sometimes cruel and hostile reception amidst anti-war rallies. He began to drink heavily."

Joanne told their history, which could have been a movie, of how they had met in 1970 and dated for four years, but his alcoholism caused them to part as friends, and of how in 1977 Jim married another woman, had a daughter, and then divorced five years later. He and Joanne were reunited by friends who thought they were meant for each other and that love would prevail. This time it did, and they married. Jim's dream was to go to Alaska. "So off we went," Joanne wrote. They headed west with all their belongings in a Ryder truck. I could imagine the adventure of it all—the planning, the goodbyes and hugs, the happy anticipation, during the long drive, of cabins in the woods and living off the land. It's what Chip and I did; it's what so many Alaskans of Jim and Joanne's generation did. Their daughter was born on Christmas Day 1989 in Juneau. They settled in Haines shortly after that. Joanne wrote that her husband loved Haines, especially salmon fishing and prospecting in the old gold-mining district near Porcupine. They had a good life here, she wrote, and she made sure we all knew that Jim took great pride in his daughters—and his military service.

WHICH BRINGS ME RIGHT back to the peace march. I had been thinking about Jim, and guys like Jim. Haines and Klukwan sent twenty-nine men to Vietnam, local boys who, thankfully, all came home. Since that time, many more vets have arrived. A lot of them don't wear veteran's caps or hang out at the Legion. This is part of the reason why, when the Haines People for Peace group announced they were planning a walk for peace on the anniversary of the start of the war in Iraq, I fretted so much about whether to attend. I didn't want to be disrespectful or inadvertently cause the kind of harm Joanne said drove Jim to drink.

Chip hadn't spent two minutes thinking about it.

When I asked him, about twelve times in one day, if he thought I should go, he always answered, "It's up to you." When I asked him if he was going, he said he'd decide when the time came. When I complained that I was so sick about the war I was thinking of moving to the Yukon, he said the snow has everyone depressed and, "It's colder up there and there's no ocean." Chip and I were by ourselves for a whole week for the first time since Eliza was born. Well, that's if you don't count the three weeks we were together in Seattle while I was in the hospital and the nursing home. (Which I don't, since we weren't exactly together, in the biblical sense: I was immobilized with an external fixator holding my bones together like a vice. It consisted of two long titanium screws drilled into my hip bones and bolted to carbon fiber rods that crossed my abdomen. For months I couldn't roll over, and in those Seattle weeks the only way I could sit up was to raise the head of the mechanical bed. After I was back in Haines, Dr. Len Feldman and Laurie Dadourian, the acu- puncturist, removed it, right there in my living room, by unbolting the rods and using them as handles to unwind the screws from the bones. One side was stuck and Len, or maybe Laurie—it is nice that I have forgotten some of those things, isn't it?—anyway, one of them had to wind the screw *back* into my hip in order to release it from the bone. It was something Hawkeye from *M*A*S*H* might do, or a scene from *The Red Badge of Courage*. I bit down on a bandana to keep from screaming and Chip held my arms down.)

As I said, that time together didn't count. But now, we really were home alone. It was spring break at school and Eliza was skiing in Utah with Christian, and Sarah was hosting her two younger sisters at Washington State University for the week. Chip and I worked in the mornings, then met for a snowshoe in the afternoon. We had dinner with a candle and a bottle of wine in the kitchen and we kissed with the bedroom door open. After months of recuperation, we were back to normal, only better. I no longer worried as much if the house was clean or if dinner was on time, and Chip had lost the tense look in his eyes he had had for a long time after the accident. He did tell me one day that he does the taxes very early now instead of waiting until the last minute, because something unforeseen could come up—although surprises as dramatic as mine are not the norm, especially at the end of a long winter.

It had been another very quiet week. I attended the Lenten retreat while Chip did a lot of sudokus. The conversations at Mountain Market and the Bamboo Room were about whether or not we would break the all-time snowfall record and what time it was, prompting Matt, the new reporter at the *Chilkat Valley News,* who had come from Ohio, to mumble, "Snow in Alaska is not news and neither is daylight savings time." The record keepers said we had only a couple of inches to go before we passed the 294-inch mark. "You figure out how many feet that is," Matt said. "I don't really care."

I think Matt may have been regretting his career choice. I know he was regretting his cabin site. The darling little shack six miles from town right on Paradise Cove had seemed like Eden in August when he had signed the winter lease. But keeping the stove stoked and hauling water had not been easy. The last big snowstorm left his truck so buried he'd been hitchhiking back and forth to the office in town. Well, mainly just forth. He hadn't been home in a week. "I'm basically couch-surfing," he said one night after dinner at our house, glancing at the soft sofa by the fire. I brought him a blanket and pillow. In the morning he said it was the most peaceful sleep he'd had in days.

Time was in the news as well, because when the rest of the nation sprung their clocks an hour ahead, the Alaska state-owned and -operated ferry system didn't. Someone forgot to make the change on the fleet's printed schedules. The ships were running from Bellingham up to Skagway and back, stopping in all the small ports along the way, on winter time. When I called to ask if the ferry from Juneau was on time, the conversation with my friend Joanne Waterman, who works at the ferry terminal, went something like this:

"Hi, Joanne."

"Hi, Heather. Staying warm?"

"Yup. Is the ferry on time?"

"Yes."

"It gets in at one thirty?"

"No, two thirty."

"I thought you said it's on time."

"It is—on the old time, dear." And then she started singing, "Does anyone really know what time it is . . ."

I should have been glad that this was the biggest gripe with the government in my world; I should have, and I would have, if it were. When I told Chip for about the tenth time that I'd made up my mind, and that I would, for sure, participate in the peace march, he said, "It won't stop the war." It also may make Haines less, rather than more, peaceful. This community is small enough to resemble a large extended family and, even though we have plenty of old protesters in the clan, we also have all those veterans: not-so-old soldiers like Jim and his friend Ron, a freelance preacher sort of guy who specializes in post-traumatic stress disorder. Ron helped Jim when he was down. He didn't cross the street to avoid him. Instead, he'd put his arm around Jim's big shoulders and suggest they get some coffee at his place. There are also local soldiers who have served, are serving, or will serve in Afghanistan and Iraq and no doubt other conflicts around the world.

I am sure there is no one here who doesn't support the troops. Of course we do. I am also sure that, even in Haines, where we do have some belligerent folks, there isn't one person who doesn't want peace. In this, I don't think we are all that different from people everywhere. When I said this to Chip, he said, "You worry too much."

At the potluck supper concluding the Lenten retreat I sought the advice of one of the Catholic participants whom I admire. He was wearing insulated canvas coveralls and a beaver fur hat. He agreed that war is terrible. He said he believed in a God who blessed peacemakers, who instructed us to love our enemies. He believed in all that Sunday school teaches. He has a teenage daughter, Nikki, who is blind, hard of hearing, and has trouble speaking and walking as a result of the recurring optical nerve cancer for which she has been treated aggressively since she was an infant. They volunteer together on the country music show on the radio one afternoon a week. It is sometimes hard to understand what Nikki is saying, but I want to so badly that I don't mind when I sometimes can't.

Nikki's dad knows a lot about the whys and wherefores of this world. He knows suffering and he knows joy. You can see both in his eyes when he speaks. With him, they aren't separate but happening at the same time. He said that walking for peace, right down the snow-packed streets in broad daylight, would be akin to "throwing the first stone" at a sinner. "I'm not going to hold myself up as some perfectly peaceful guy," he said. "I'll pray for peace instead."

I decided to consult another authority on peace. I have a thin volume on faith by the Buddhist monk Thich Nhat Hanh that I consult occasionally when I'm spiritually stuck. He writes that we have to make peace in our hearts before we can make world peace. Great. Just thinking about peace had conflicted my heart for the better part of a week.

THE DAY BEFORE THE WALK, I finally made up my mind not to participate. Chip and I were on a long snowshoe deep in the woods on Mt. Ripinsky. It was so peaceful, so snowy and quiet: just us and spruce and hemlock trees so old and twisted they could have been Little Red Riding Hood's forest. I knew that the Buddhist monk and Nikki's dad were right. This was my peace march. God wouldn't hear my cries any louder on Main Street than he would right here. Besides, who am I to stand up for peace when I am so easily ticked at school board budget meetings? Sometimes I think I'm not cut out for my service on the school board. Just last week the mayor advocated cutting the school budget, which may mean no more sports, including my beloved cross-country. It was terrible news, and I didn't take it well. Also, that new guy who walks everywhere and comes to all the school board meetings was there. I'm not sure who he is or where he's from but every time I speak, I have the impression he thinks I'm as dumb as a post and I'm tired of it. When I asked Father Bob about how to handle such an unpleasant person, he said there must be a reason why the man is so contrary. He suggested that the next time he speaks to the school board, I should look at him and repeat to myself: "Everyone needs to be needed, wants to be wanted, and loves to be loved." He also quoted Thomas Merton, reminding me that mature spirituality is making the connections between our faith and the world we live in. Just like passing the peace in church, I thought. We don't exchange it telepathically; we walk around and grab hands and sometimes hug that peace right into someone else's heart.

The morning of the peace walk, Chip and I went to a St. Patrick's Day breakfast at Don and Becky's house. It was their son Aaron's thirtieth birthday, and we were having green eggs and ham with about a dozen members of the extended Nash family and their friends. Aaron had been on my running team in high school; he was also a basketball player and one of the most gifted artists ever to graduate from Linnus's Haines High art class. Linnus and I both wrote him recommendations to an art school in Washington State. They offered him a scholarship, but he never quite made it there. In fact, he hasn't quite moved out of his parents' home, remaining in Haines, drawing and painting some, fishing with his father, and working in his brother Song's restaurant. It is hard to believe he is thirty already. I sat next to Don and Becky's grandson, Ocean. I am Ocean's fairy godmother. He doesn't have a real godmother, because his parents do not attend church. Don and Becky, who raised Ocean's dad to believe in the God of Sunday mornings, daily devotions, and Presbyterian hymns, have adjusted.

In the same way that the Second Song of Isaiah, which we chant in plainsong at our church each Sunday during Lent, reminds us, Becky believes that God's ways are not our ways, and that His power and love are doing infinitely more than we can imagine. Although Becky probably wouldn't say it that way. She'd probably shrug, open her big blue eyes wide, smile, and say, "Stuff happens."

When Don and Becky's son Lee and his girlfriend,

Shannah, asked to borrow our double kayak years before, I had said sure and had collected the paddles and spray skirts and helped them lift the boat onto the top of their truck. I had had no hint of their impending good accident, just as I had had none about my bad one. No women's intuition at all that a new life was about to begin, that Becky's first grandchild was about to be conceived. Six weeks after that overnight camping trip, when Shannah and Lee told Becky they were expecting, Becky was so happy she had to sit down. When they decided to name the baby Ocean, no matter what gender it turned out to be, Becky was so moved she had to lie down.

When Ocean was a little over two years old, his parents were married on the beach not far from our house. Jesse McGraw officiated. The red-haired local basketball star works for the phone company now, but he had been a deckhand on the Nash family fishing boat when it sank, and he had saved Lee's and Song's lives by holding on to them throughout the night until the Coast Guard helicopter arrived and plucked them out of the ocean, which, as I've mentioned before, claimed the life of their little brother, Olen.

At the wedding, Don thanked us all for coming, then said it was fitting that Jesse was officiating, because without him there would be no marriage to celebrate, and no Ocean, because there would be no Lee. Of course, we all cried happy and sad tears. We couldn't help it. This was such a good ending to such a tragic tale. Except that it was not the end. Life at the Nash house, and at yours and mine, with any luck at all, keeps rolling along. We love, we fight, we make mistakes, we change, and we redeem ourselves. As Satchel Paige said, "Sometimes you win, sometimes you lose, and sometimes it rains." Or, as Father Bob said, when a creationist asked him what he thought about Darwin, "Of course I believe in evolution. I don't care if you are a single-cell animal or a bishop, if you don't change, you die."

On St. Patrick's Day, in his high chair next to me, Ocean was eating ham and coffee cake. He didn't like the green eggs. For his uncle Aaron's birthday, Ocean had carefully wrapped a can of tuna fish. He kept tossing it at Aaron, who, much to Ocean's delight, "caught the fish" again and again. Ocean has a great vocabulary for a three-year-old. He has been taught to use words to solve problems and that hitting is wrong. His parents have never spanked him. Ocean lives in a peaceful family, and he has made a real kind of peace with everyone who loves him and that family. He should inherit a world that has outgrown using guns and bombs to hurt or kill people. He should never have to go war like Jim did—or return from one to face the challenges he did, either. No one should.

And that is why after breakfast I joined about thirty folks and walked around town for peace. I think it also may be why Chip came with me. For all my worries, no one who drove by seemed to mind us, and some people beeped in support. Chip's goat-hunting friend Ed was even there. Old Ed learned how to survive in the mountains during his childhood in warring and later Nazi-occupied Poland. In his accented English, he said he was walking today because, "Watching the news on television, it sometimes makes me so sad tears come."

AFTER JOANNE'S LETTER was read at that veterans' dinner at the Legion, there was a moment of silence, then applause, and more applause, and finally a standing ovation. Old veterans wiped their eyes, while wives, sweethearts, and daughters wept more openly. I suppose it could be argued that our little Haines peace walk was a lot of fuss for nothing, that no one important paid any attention. As Chip had said, it didn't stop the war. It wasn't televised. Anderson Cooper didn't cover it. It made the *Chilkat Valley News* because Tom was there with a notebook and a camera, but that's about it. And for certain it would be even easier to argue that the world isn't any more peaceful now just because we willed it to be, for a little bit of one day, the same way it can be argued that making one child smile doesn't make the world a happier place. I beg to differ, though. All you have to do is toss Ocean a can of tuna fish and watch him laugh as he "catches the fish" to see that that is not true.

CHAPTER 12

Muerte Beach

So teach us
to number our days.
—Psalm 90

Y ou could blame the three recent Haines weddings in
Hawaii on what happens when sun, heat, and fresh-
fruit-starved Alaskans fly from the bitter cold and darkness into the bright light of warm tropical beaches in the
middle of February. Sue Nelson and Tim June were in Hawaii to attend one of the other local weddings when they
decided to go ahead and get married themselves. It was
so spur-of-the-moment that Sue didn't have time to buy
a dress or invite many of her close friends. They found a
minister in the phone book, called her up, explained that
they were thinking about getting married but weren't going to be in Hawaii much longer, and hoped it could be
done that day. The minister wanted a little more information. She was concerned about vacationers rushing into

something as important as marriage. She knew that tropical paradise has a way of making normally cool-headed (not to mention cold-footed) Alaskans behave recklessly. She was also well aware that half of all marriages end in divorce and was doing her part to make sure the unions she blessed batted a little closer to 1,000. She suggested that Tim and Sue wait until they knew each other better. Maybe they could return to Hawaii next year for a properly planned wedding.

That's when Tim said that he and Sue had been sweethearts since junior high. They had lived together since they were in college. They had been in love for thirty-six years.

The minister begged to marry them. It would be wonderful to preside at a ceremony for a couple who had already tested and survived the better and worse, sickness and health, and richer and poorer parts of the vows and still had no quarrels with any of it. Even if they hadn't had all that going for them, it would have been very hard to turn down Sue and Tim if she had met them in person. Sue is pretty, blonde, quick to smile, laughs as much as Tim does, and is just so kind to everyone. She is as apolitical as Tim is political. And Tim, well, as my friend and editor Tom says, "What's not to like about a guy who is thrilled about waking up each morning? It's fun to be around someone who is never having a bad day."

I had hoped that Tim and Sue would get married when we were together in Mexico. The Thanksgiving after my

accident I had gone there with them and a group of mothers and our daughters and single women. It was officially
a women's trip, but Tim came along, too, and because
Tim is Tim, everyone was fine with it. Besides, it was a
good idea to have one man around as a chaperone, especially one who speaks Spanish fluently and has a way
of making friends with everyone from the local guy who
drives the water truck to the couple from Beverly Hills
renting the house next door.

I like being home. I don't have any urge to see foreign
shores. I come from the Dorothy school of life: everything
I am looking for is right in my own backyard. Unlike
George Bailey, I don't pine for the sound of train whistles
or ship horns. But Tim, as I've said, is hard to say no to.
Even more so when you are flat on your back and taking
large doses of morphine, as I was that May when he and
Sue and everyone else talked me into the trip.

The first morning in Mexico I asked my friend Lisa
what time it was. "Who cares?" she said. She was wearing a big yellow straw hat, a small blue and yellow bikini,
and Audrey Hepburn sunglasses. She looked like a movie
star. She's a first-grade teacher in an international school
in Korea. She and her husband used to teach in Alaska;
now they return to their Haines cabin each summer. I
had asked Lisa what time it was because I was wondering when lunch was. "If you're hungry, go eat," Lisa said.
"This is Mexico. Relax."

A few weeks earlier, Chip and I had been sitting by

the fire, listening to the north wind blow, when he asked, "What do people do on vacation in Mexico?" I said they probably go to the beach. "That's all? They just do nothing?" He couldn't quite wrap his hardworking Norwegian heart around that one. Then he predicted, "You won't like it very much." I had already bought the tickets. J.J.'s and Stoli's flip-flops, swimsuits, and shorts were packed. (Their older sisters were taking trips of their own.) My friends were even reminding me to buy precautions like charcoal tablets. "So you won't get sick," Anna said. "The charcoal absorbs toxins in the water."

Toxins in the water?

Now Chip and our son were in a wall tent on the edge of a snowy cove on a wilderness island south of Haines, and my friends and I were a few thousand miles farther down the same coast in a rented beach house in Sayulita, a fishing and tourist town not all that different from home. Well, except for the weather and the palm trees and the soft, ripe avocados.

Tim became Timiteo once he was south of the border, and in his faded tropical shorts and sandals he looked the part of an expatriate American right out of a Jimmy Buffett song. (He reminds me of Mark that way; they are both free-spirited, beach-loving guys.) His hair seemed to be longer, curlier, and lighter than when we'd left, although close up those highlights were gray, just like mine. Every time we walked the dusty trail to town I'd look at him and hum, "Down to the Banana Republics, things aren't as warm as they seem . . ." or "Wasting away again in Margaritaville . . ." I was surprised one afternoon when he put on his half-glasses to read. Is that my friend Tim, I wondered, or a friend of my dad's? Are we twenty-five or fifty? Where did the years go? But rather than be sad about time passing, I was grateful to be there, and pleased that both Tim and I had made it that far. We've both had close calls.

TIM AND SUE have been a couple so long that it's rare to use their names singularly. They are mostly "Tim and Sue," or the even shorter and more intertwined "Sim-Tue," which is also the name of Tim's boat-building and carpentry business. Tim can do just about anything he puts his mind to, except win a seat in the Alaska state house or senate. His Republican opponents have labeled him an "extreme environmentalist," and in Alaska that is not a compliment. It is a tribute to Tim's good nature that his races are as close as they are. Even his political enemies like him.

Tim taught himself how to be a cabinetmaker, a wood-carver, a boat builder, and a commercial fisherman. He can repair a diesel engine, wire solar panels and wind generators, plumb a bathroom, and give a public policy speech to a crowded convention center. He is as comfortable in paint-splattered coveralls with two days' worth of stubble on his face as he is in khakis and a tweed blazer looking like your favorite high school English teacher.

214 | TAKE GOOD CARE OF THE GARDEN AND THE DOGS

When we were building our house, he was the one who figured out how to design and construct the staircase.

Tim and Sue have been at our holiday dinners for twenty years. When the children were small, Sue slept over on Christmas Eve because she wanted to be there when they woke up, stumbled out of bed in their pajamas, and saw the magic of the tree surrounded by gifts. (At our house there are no presents in sight until Christmas morning. Chip and I hide them in our bedroom and set them out after midnight mass.)

On Sue's fortieth birthday, quite a few years back now, Tim rented the Haines Senior Center and organized a family board-game party. Everyone who came in the door had to fill out a name tag as a Nelson because, Tim said, Sue always wanted a big family that played games together. So he gave her one: all of us. Tim and Sue never had children because Tim's cancer treatments had made him infertile. He was nineteen years old when he was diagnosed with Hodgkin's disease. Two-thirds of the way through debilitating radiation treatments his doctors suggested he save some sperm because the next round might harm his ability to reproduce. After what Tim called "the weird and humiliating" sperm bank visit, he learned that the treatments had already killed his future babies. It was a surprise to his doctors.

This had a lot to do with the decision Tim made a few weeks later. He was sitting in a hospital room while the same team of physicians marked him up with tattoo targets for radiation beams. While they worked on him, they talked about cameras. Tim was a pretty good photographer in those days. (No doubt you've gathered by now that Tim is pretty good at anything he takes an interest in.) One of the doctors was talking about his own new camera, a Yashica 35mm. He said it was the best one money could buy. At the time, Nikons were the industry standard. Tim knew that. "So I'm sitting there, listening to them, and thinking, they can afford any camera they want and this guy buys a Yashica? He doesn't know enough to buy a good camera, so how's he going to cure me?"

It reminded me of the comment my mother made when the space shuttle exploded. She'd said, "I'm not surprised. I can't even find anyone who knows how to fix the toaster."

So Tim left. He left the hospital, his parents' home, and Sue (or at least the nearness of her—she was finishing college) and headed for the clean air and fresh water of the San Bernardino Mountains, where he restored his body and soul and began living as if he were dying. Then he came to Alaska, where he was convinced that the environment could save him, or at least buy him some years. His doctors had promised him that if he finished the treatments he had an 85 percent chance of surviving. If he walked away, they said, he wouldn't live six months.

TIM IS FIFTY-FOUR NOW. He is sitting at my kitchen table. We are having leftover chicken and pesto for lunch. I had been trying to get him to build another bookcase in our living room for three years. Don Nash ended up making it instead, and he had just installed it before Tim came by with his notebook and tape measure. When I showed him it was already finished, Tim laughed. "Oh, good, I really didn't have the time anyway." But he was not too busy to stay for lunch. He never is. He spends his days doing what he wants to do rather than things he needs to do. His belief that his cancer was caused in large part by environmental pollution has spurred him to devote his time to campaigning for the environment, especially for clean air and water. He does most of it for free, though he is neither retired nor independently wealthy. He gets by. Sue's part-time job supports them both, and the small carpentry jobs he squeezes in between the hours he spends saving the world help. He does have a fishing boat and fishes commercially when he isn't too busy. Some summers he is more successful than others.

Tim drops everything, though, if a friend gets sick, especially with cancer. He offers guidance and support; he researches all the options; he sits in hospital rooms in Seattle; he asks the doctors questions and listens very carefully to their answers. He built my wheelchair ramps, and he visited my recovery bed. Often. It is always good to see Tim. When he was running for the legislature, I hosted a fundraiser. I had never even attended a political fundraiser before and, while I lean left of center, I'm not as far over as Tim. But I would rather have a friend in Juneau than someone I don't know at all, someone who might not listen or who might not have the courage to disagree with me, the way I know Tim would. For a gentle-mannered guy, he can be pretty gutsy.

When Tim wants to attract the attention of a mining company or cruise-line official who argues that there is such a thing as an acceptable limit to the waste they can burn, bury, or discharge into the land, air, or water, he will take off his shirt and show the scar where his chest was peeled open in order to remove half a lung. Then he asks which part per billion would be okay if it killed your son, your wife, or your neighbor? But when we were in Mexico and someone asked about the same scar, Tim just said, "Shark bite, great white," and laughed.

Tim is an active member of Lynn Canal Conservation (the Haines environmental group), the Southeast Alaska Conservation Council, and the Alaska Marine Conservation Council; a spokesman for Alaska Community Action on Toxics; and a founder of the Alaska Clean Water Alliance. He worked for former Alaska governor Tony Knowles as an environmental policy adviser. In between meetings and public hearings he has built a small, creative Victorian-style home for Sue and him at Paradise Cove (well, actually he is still building it), along with the alternative solar and wind systems that power it. His old Toyota Land Cruiser may soon be running on French fry grease from the Bamboo Room.

• • •

AFTER TIM BECAME SICK, everything changed for the then teen sweethearts Tim and Sue. They had planned to marry after college and live in the sunshine of their Southern California youth. Tim had even thought about going to the U.S. Air Force Academy. Instead he traveled to Haines to work with a friend on a wood-carving project at Alaska Indian Arts. Lee Heinmiller, who now runs AIA as his father did before him, met Tim at the ferry terminal in a February snowstorm. The snow was coming down so thick and fast that they couldn't even see the mountains, but Tim said it was love at first deep breath. "It was the first time I felt at home in my life," he told me. What home meant had changed because Tim had. He had walked into the hospital an athletic nineteen-year-old and left moving like a feeble-bodied eighty-year-old. His startling free fall from healthy to half-dead taught him early that everyone could be just a checkup away from the same fate. People in wheelchairs, homeless people, sick people, and dying people, Tim realized, were all the same as him. It was a revelation to a California golden boy. Thanks to cancer, he had gained (and has kept) the wisdom and compassion of a much older man.

After graduating from college, Sue joined Tim in Haines, and they embarked on a life together defined by his illness. They lived hour-to-hour, day-to-day. The main thing was that they were together and making the most of Tim's brief time left on earth. They lucked into jobs longshoring, where they worked three or four days a month and made enough cash to eat and pay rent. They fished, picked berries, baked bread, and made their own yogurt. "All we wanted to do was to be with each other and have fun," Tim said. They hoped he'd make it to thirty.

Sue found a job in the borough office and Tim started building a sailboat, working on it whenever he could. It was, he said, "Plan C." Plan A had been curing his cancer and Plan B had been skipping the cure to move to Alaska. When the cancer caught up with him—they both assumed it would—Tim planned to sail off into the sunrise and never return. You can't sail very far into the sunset out of Haines without running into the side of a fjord. If you want to leave local waters you have to head south and east down Lynn Canal between steep mountains. Tim decided to create a reproduction of L. Francis Herreshoff's thirty-six-foot ketch, *Nereia,* a grand pleasure boat from the heyday of sailing yachts. "It was my meditation, my coffin, my ark," he says now, fairly quietly.

It took him longer than Noah had to build it, about nine and a half years. He milled the yellow cedar for the hull and then dried and planed it. He collected old lead from car batteries and weights and melted it down for the keel. He cast the bronze fittings, sewed the sails, scavenged portholes and cabin skylights. The *Keku,* named for the perfume Sue wore in junior high, looks as though it belongs in Newport, rather than tied up between the fishing boats in the Haines harbor. Her dark green hull, glossy varnished trim, cream-colored cabin, fir decks, boldly raked Sitka spruce masts, and carved bowsprit, are all, as our friend and road construction company owner Roger Schnabel says, "very impressive."

After the boat was launched, at a big party at Letnikof Cove, out by the cannery, with Roger driving the front-end loader that gently lowered the trailer with the *Keku* on it down the ramp and into the water; after Sue had christened it with a bottle of champagne and everyone cheered; after Tim had motored it around the peninsula to the harbor in front of town and stepped the masts and rigged the halyards, carefully following the designer's specifications; after just about everything was done except the curtains hung on the portholes in the main salon, Tim asked me if I'd help teach him to sail.

His first test was the Juneau Yacht Club's "Spirit of Adventure" race, which took place over the summer solstice. Tim, Alex—a sailing friend from California—and I took turns at the helm and trimming the sails. The two-hundred-mile course begins and ends in Juneau and circles the Admiralty Island National Monument. The island's Tlingit name, *Kootznoowoo,* means "Fortress of the Bears." It is where Chip and Christian and Roger and his boys had set up their wall tent to hunt deer while the rest of us were in Mexico. In a good year the sailboat race takes about three days, including a mandatory lay-over at Baranof Warm Springs, a tiny almost-ghost town with natural hot springs where we all soaked in metal horse troughs set in the fast-moving steamy creek. Tim,

Alex, and I put our swimsuits on, climbed into one of the horse troughs, ducked down so just our heads were showing and it looked like we were nude, and took a picture, joking that we should send it as a Christmas card and make everyone wonder what happened to my family, Sue, and Alex's girlfriend. "Let's give them something to talk about," Tim said.

The *Keku* was the star of the regatta, mainly because she was so beautiful, so old-fashioned, and so sturdy. People couldn't believe Tim had built her. She's the kind of sailboat that helps you understand why boats are referred to in the feminine. She's also the kind of boat sailors dream of but take one look at and say they'd never have time for the upkeep—all that wood, varnish, and brass. Everyone wondered how Tim could afford it and where he found the time to build and maintain it. Tim smiled and shrugged. He and Sue had lived in a rented room upstairs at Alaskan Indian Arts during the years Tim was working on the boat. His other car isn't a Bentley; it's that rusty Toyota.

Other crews were wet and cold from the spray and wind and relying on freeze-dried meals, while we were sitting high and dry on a cushioned bench in the cozy cockpit with a turkey breast roasting in the big oil stove in the galley below. The strong winds during the first leg worked in our favor as the long, heavy hull cut smoothly into the waves.

Late, or early, in the twilight of the second, or maybe

third day, somewhere around two or three in the morning, the sky turned all orangey-pink and lavender, and it was as if sunrise and sunset had combined. It never did get dark on this longest day of the year. We were a little sleepy. Although we had promised one another to rest and work in traditional four-hour watches, we didn't. None of us wanted to miss anything, from the chance of seeing a pod of killer whales to the moonrise over the snow-capped mountains. Also, when it became clear how well Tim's boat could sail, and that with the handicap rating we might even win the race, we started actively competing: trimming and retrimming and changing headsails, tacking for better angles, adjusting the draft of the mainsail and the mizzen and working the tides and currents to our best advantage. Tim may not have had as much experience sailing as Alex and I did, but he knew the area well from his years fishing. We were a good team.

It was sometime in that gorgeous dusky middle-of-the-night dawn, when the wind died down and we coasted quietly with our biggest jib gently tugging at the lines, as water lapped the hull, and it was so quiet and so lovely, that Tim asked if I believed in soul mates, if I thought one's partner in life was predetermined. I said I wasn't sure—that it was a chicken and egg kind of thing. If you think someone is your soul mate, you'll make it so. Tim said he thought it was something determined before you were born.

· · ·

Tɪᴍ ᴀɴᴅ Sᴜᴇ may have wed in Hawaii, but they still had a Haines reception. The theme, naturally, was tropical, with fabric leis, flowered shirts, and sticky blender drinks. Tom from the paper and his wife, Jane, hosted the bash at a friends' house. The owners were on vacation, and Tom and Jane had come down from their cabin in the woods, which has no running water and is a long snowshoe from the road, to house-sit. (Here's where Jane will say, "We have running water—we have to run and get it.") On the deck, out in single-digit temperatures, the grill was smoking away with halibut kabobs. In the living room, two laptops ran slide shows of all three local but Hawaiian weddings. While I was interested in the others, I soaked up the pictures of the most mature newlyweds. Sue blushed. Tim beamed.

Tim is used to smiling at weddings. He has married a few people in that Alaska way in which anyone can be made a marriage commissioner for a day. I have even done it, officiating at the marriage of my friend Linnus's daughter. Tim has been asked often, because of his long relationship with Sue, his sense of humor, and his thoughtful but not preachy manner. More recently, he has also conducted difficult memorial services for two of his neighbors. Unlike a wedding, this does not require a license, only a willing heart and the ability to keep your voice strong when others can't. One friend died too young of cancer, another, Guy Hoffman, of a heart attack while skiing on Chilkoot Lake. At both Tim made the stunned mourners laugh through tears. When he addressed us all at Guy's service in the Chilkat Center for the Arts auditorium, Tim began with a paper bag full of props. He pulled out a feather duster he had found at Guy's rustic, or let's just say, "well lived-in," Mud Bay Road home. It was still in the wrapper. Guy, a woodworker known around Alaska for his lathe-turned and sometimes colorfully painted birch bowls and platters, underwrote a jazz show on the radio, and each time it was broadcast his motto, "One good turn deserves another," was read by the announcer. His friends and family buried him in his front yard, overlooking the horseshoe pit and, in the distance, Rainbow Glacier.

A group of woodworkers, including Tim, built Guy's casket and then elaborately carved the lid. Tim said it was good work to do. They planted a birch tree on top of the grave and festooned the branches with a string of colorful Tibetan prayer flags. Buddhists believe that every time the flags flutter, the prayers written on them disperse in the breeze. They also believe that anyone touched by the prayer-bearing wind will live long, be happy, and have good fortune. It makes you wonder if those sails Tim sewed so carefully had caught the prayers from all the faded flags dancing on all the old hippie porches and trees and rafters from California to Alaska. It makes you wonder if Tim knew that by playing in the wind he'd receive those prayers.

Tim and Guy had also been in the local swing band

together. Tim is the drummer and Guy was the clarinet player for Lunchmeat and the Pimientos. When it was time for Guy's eulogy, Tim took off his coat, tie, and oxford cloth shirt—what I call his running-for-office outfit—and revealed a faded tropical Hawaiian shirt, just like Guy always wore on stage.

I have a feeling it may have been the funerals over which Tim officiated, more than the weddings, that prompted "the Junesons," as some friends are now calling Tim and Sue, to marry after all these years. There is something about burying a friend that makes you want to declare what is most important to you in life, and if you are fortunate, that is true love. Also, when Guy died, Tim realized that he really and truly had survived his cancer. While he was waiting to die, he had managed to live a very full life. He figures even if the Hodgkin's disease returned tomorrow, it would not be a tragedy if it killed him; it would be almost normal. So why not just get married and make something that he and Sue had always believed in official?

The good news was that when he finally asked Sue, she said yes. At their wedding reception, which was more of a big midwinter party in their honor, Tom made up his own version of the old *Newlywed Game* TV show, in which spouses answer questions the way they think their mates would. It was not just for Tim and Sue. Every married couple at the party played. But they won. When Tom asked Sue if Tim were a car, would he be a Lexus or a VW van, Sue answered that Tim was the van all the way. That was an easy guess, since everyone at the party was more van than luxury car. Mark Sebens does have that old Mercedes, but I'm not sure it still runs. Tim clinched it when he knew the answer to Tom's question, "Where was your first kiss?" as well as the month, day, and year of it. That would be Sue's mother's front porch, January 7, 1970.

I DON'T EVEN REMEMBER the exact dates that Tim and Sue and I were all in Mexico. But I do know that the waves in front of the house we shared were huge, and about all we could do was dive into the curl and pop up on the other side, bob around, and try to get out again without being smashed into the sand. This was hard on my joints and a little scary for my recovering psyche, so we found another beach where I could float or snorkel gently all day long. It was about a half-hour walk, past town, and up and over a dirt road that cut through a cemetery. The soft, sandy cove with gentle waves was called baby beach, because it was the best place to take small children, or *muerte* beach, because it was next to the graveyard. The names reminded me of those yoga poses—the birth and the corpse positions we do so close to each other in our routine.

On our last night in Sayulita, Timiteo mixed up margaritas, Sue cut up a pineapple, and we ate and drank on the lawn overlooking the beach, as the surf crashed and the wind through the palm trees sounded a little like rain. The evening light on sun-tanned skin made everyone look beatific. Chip was wrong. I loved doing nothing in Mexico, and so did J.J. and Stoli. I didn't miss home or even the rest of my family. I could have stayed at least another week. I could have stayed a month. While we were partying, a woman came walking down the beach, looked up at us, and waved. It was Miss Patty Brown, a teacher from Haines who, in one of those small-world coincidences, had also been vacationing there. We invited her to join us, and she climbed up the stone steps from the beach to the terrace.

I looked at Tim and Sue, and my friends and our daughters, and I thought maybe Tim had died from his cancer. Maybe I had died. Maybe *muerte* beach, the beach of the dead, is another name for heaven. On the other hand, I thought, maybe I should quit drinking tequila. But what if that teacher who just walked in had left earth altogether and didn't even know it? Maybe Guy would be showing up with his clarinet soon. If being bathed in light perpetual means spending eternity with your friends and family in a place like this — with some showing up sooner and others arriving later — it's not nearly as scary as I had thought. When I think of heaven now, I hear the surf and feel the sun.

THERE IS ANOTHER LESSON to be learned from Tim. Since he is no longer living as if he is dying, he has become more like the rest of us. He spends more time away from home and Sue, speaking out on environmental issues with an evangelical's zeal. The guy who lived all those days as if each one were his last has been spending a lot more of them doing things that aren't all that much fun, such as flying to Anchorage for tough talks with politicians and executives from oil and mining companies. That's really why he couldn't build my bookshelves. Over lunch in my kitchen now he mentions a recent Ninth Circuit Court of Appeals ruling against a proposal to dump gold-mine waste into a lake between Haines and Juneau. Then he says, "I tell Sue that this is all bonus time now." And when I ask if he minds the meetings and letter writing, he says, "I'm doing what I'm doing because I believe in it." He looks so stern I hardly recognize him. But it lasts only a minute. Then he laughs. "Radical stuff, huh?" he says, and reaching for more chicken, asks, "So when are we going back to Mexico? Man, that was fun."

CHAPTER 13

Amazing Grace

Forgive us our trespasses
as we forgive those who trespass against us.
—The Lord's Prayer

A dozen of us had a ski race one Saturday at the snow machine track twenty-five miles out on the Haines Highway. My friend Liam, who helps coach the cross-country team with me these days, organized it and had changed the location earlier in the week when it looked as though the April sunshine and warm wind would make the snow too soft on the golf course, where we had been skiing all winter. Standing in a foot of fresh snow on race day, with still more coming down, he joked, "We're out here today because there's too much snow in town." There is usually less snow in the coastal townsite this time of year than farther up the colder Chilkat Valley toward Canada. But on this particular morning, there was a surprise—shin-deep wet snow blanketed roads, yards, and rooftops from Front Street to Officer's Row. Of course, it was snowing hard up the valley, too. (Maybe you don't need to know this, maybe the weather is an inside joke. Still, we thought it was funny to drive twenty-five miles on a yet unplowed road for a race we could practically have run on Main Street.) The spring blizzard didn't quit until the next day, a few hours before the Blessing of the Fleet after church on Palm Sunday.

The ski race, a relay, required four teams of four to ski loops around the oval. (Yes, you are correct—there were not enough of us to field that many teams so Liam skied extra laps.) There were no rules regarding skating or classic styles, either. But it was not a free-for-all. The entry fee was a donation to the Hospice of Haines community cancer treatment travel fund. Without a hospital, residents have to leave town to treat serious illnesses, often heading as far as Seattle. It is hard to be alone at a time like that but costly to have visitors. This fund helps pay for a patient's airfare and for a family member or friend to accompany them.

A dog musher who had once played college football made sure both skiers had stopped before slapping palms for a hand-off, which lead to a few face-plants in the tag zone. I did not fall when my teammate hit my hand, and neither did the physical therapist I raced against. Dr. Marnie Hartman is the only practicing physical therapist in Haines. She helped me learn to walk again and, more important, to find the confidence to run, ski, and cycle after my terrible accident. Marnie made house calls when I first came home from the hospital and the Sleepless in Seattle Nursing Home and I was confined to my bed or wheelchair. The clinic had hired her a week before I was hurt; until then, there had been no physical therapist in town. (And you wonder where my faith comes from?)

Marnie is petite and blonde, and looks about twenty-five but has to be older. She was not easy on me. Sometimes, when she massaged my nerve-damaged right leg, I'd cry. She also wouldn't let me call it my "bad leg." She said if I started doing that, it would never heal. When she insisted I was ready to use a walker and showed me how to stand up leaning on it, I was afraid I'd fall. Under the watchful eyes of my caregivers — there was always someone with me in those days — slowly and steadily, I managed laps around my living room. About forty of them. The next day I was in so much pain I couldn't sit up, much less stand, with or without the walker. After that Marnie was more specific about my independent exercise, but I knew she was pleased that I was, as she would say, "going for it."

I couldn't help thinking about that as we both skied onto the course, unable to see clearly in the whiteout. I suppose we could have agreed to stay together; we could have finished holding hands. We could have, but that's not why she, and so many others, willed (and cooked and prayed) me back to health. They expected more from me. I tell young runners who Liam and I coach on the high school cross-country team to give their all in even the smallest race, reminding them that they've taken an unspoken oath to do the best that is within them.

Inspirational speeches aside, I hadn't planned to find out who I really was that Saturday. What if I poked my eye out with a ski pole or hit my head on a snow-covered log? What if I couldn't go fast enough? I also had a pretty good excuse, or at least a good reason to be cautious. It was four years ago, almost to the day (Thursday, April 7, 2005, at about 11:30 a.m., to be specific) that I was run over by the truck and broke my pelvis in six places.

I'm fine most of the time, but in April I tend to become a little wiggy. I went to my regular doctor the other day because the dentist who I saw in case I had fatal gum disease (he never even mentioned it, but I had no cavities) had noticed a slightly swollen lymph node in my neck. I was already practicing how I'd respond to the words "terminal cancer" when my doctor noted that the last time I saw him was exactly a year ago. Then, I had thought I had a blood clot in my knee (I didn't). Now, Dr. Feldman smiled and said, "See any pattern here?"

I had come to the ski race with my husband because if people don't attend events like this, we won't have them. Chip had his fancy racing skis. I purposely brought my old touring ones with the three-pin bindings. When is it okay to decide that you don't need to do your best? That you have built enough character for one lifetime? I slid up alongside Marnie and we waited for our teammates to tag us. They were skiing side by side, racing hard. I joked that I hoped I wouldn't fall down right away. Marnie smiled, said she did, too, then took off, all business, making sure we raced as if it were the Olympics. I finished with a pounding heart, gasping for air. Here's what I learned: shared experiences alone are not enough to make a community; as Wayne had said about raising that totem pole, you have to put your heart into them.

THIS IS PART OF the reason I went to the Blessing of the Fleet for the first time in a couple of years the next afternoon even though I knew it would be painful. The blessing has actually happened now for four years in a row, so maybe it finally *is* annual—which doesn't mean they've all been exactly the same. This year, the weather felt closer to October than April, and since it was Palm Sunday, palms replaced the hot-house carnations of previous years. There was fresh snow on the breakwater, and low gray clouds obscured the mountains. It was so still the harbor could have been slate. An eagle whistled from the top of a piling, appearing higher thanks to the very low tide. I really didn't have an option not to attend, since our women's choir was singing two anthems, our old standby "Dona Nobis Pacem" and "God Be in My Head," which was written by a well-known English church composer, John Rutter. The words were from a thirteenth-century Church of England book of prayer and meditation, the Sarum Primer. "God be in my head and in my understanding," it began, and continued, "God be in my eyes and in my looking. God be in my mouth and in my speaking. God be in my heart and in my thinking. God be at mine end and at my departing."

After we sang, I listened as Father Blaney from the Catholic church, dressed in his Sunday black, with a white collar under a blue and white ski jacket, read all the names of the people who died last year, the first part of this year, and ever—at seas, or in our lakes, rivers, and ponds. There were, as always, more than you'd think. Father, as he is usually called, is an outdoorsy guy. He had been serving some of the other smaller communities using a mission boat, the *Mater Dei* (Mother of God), but is back in Haines again. I would not have been surprised to see him at the race yesterday, but he was probably busy preparing for Holy Week. Marnie knows how much she helped me recover, but watching him at the blessing, I realized that Father Blaney doesn't have a clue about how much he influenced my decision to ride a bicycle fast again.

AS IT HAD BEEN with the ski race, I hadn't planned on it. But a visit from my dad, dinner with Father, and a few words from a tough old gold miner prompted me to do something I thought I didn't want to do ever again. It's not that I was afraid. A year and a half after the accident, I was riding my clunky town cruiser on errands all summer, with no jitters. Sure, I did go through even the quietest of intersections cautiously, but that's normal.

Okay, most of the time I got off and walked the bike across the street.

Because of his assignments, I hadn't seen Father Blaney since before I was injured, so when I had heard he was back in Haines to celebrate the anniversary of the founding of the Sacred Heart Catholic Church, I had invited him over for dinner. That night, he asked if the new priest could come, too, and since I was having all their clergy, I called up some other Catholics and made a party of it.

Father wanted to know all about my wreck. I have told the story a lot, and it becomes harder, not easier. But I do like him, and he enjoys a good yarn with a happy ending, and this is certainly one, so I told it again. Since he is a priest and I was among believers, I also confessed that even though I didn't hear or see God, I'm pretty sure that I felt something the equivalent of that peace we talk about in church, the one that "passes all understanding." When the truck ran over me, I wasn't scared to death; instead, I was calm enough to tense my stomach muscles as the tire hit me and order friends at the scene not to move me. I am usually such a chicken; even as I was doing all that, I felt like a different person. Something or someone changed me. A holy spirit took over. But I couldn't articulate that so well, so I told Father I suspected divine intervention. He said I was right to think so. "But," I wanted to ask, "why didn't God intervene with my mother—or in bigger disasters, such as hurricanes, tsunamis, drunk-driving accidents, or the war in Iraq?" I also wanted to ask him if he thought people who are knocked out on morphine, they way my mother had been those last days, could feel the peace of God, or if that, too, was masked by the painkillers?

That was so personal and . . . what's the word? Simplistic? Naive? Just plain dumb? It reminded me of that T. R. Pearson novel, *A Short History of a Small Place,* where the boy believes that God can't see through buildings, so it was all right to do bad things indoors. Rather than voice these questions, I changed the subject to Father's cycling. Was he still riding his bike in Hoonah, Wrangell, and the other small towns and villages here in southeast Alaska to which he's been ministering since he left Haines? "Absolutely," he said, in his loud Boston accent. "I rode out to Chilkoot Lake today." That was a twenty-mile round trip from the rectory. It had been windy that day, too—so windy that we had moved our planned beach picnic supper indoors. Riding a bicycle into the wind is twice as hard as walking or running into it.

Father Blaney must be seventy. He broke his pelvis in a car wreck decades ago. "I was T-boned," he said. He was in his twenties when he, too, spent months recuperating. Doctors were so concerned he might not survive that he was given "last rites, the whole bit." I asked if he's sometimes afraid it could happen again. "Sure, but what are you gonna do? You have to drive."

The conversation shifted as we made our way through grilled salmon, roasted potatoes and beets, garden salad, and finally rhubarb pie. Later, after everyone had gone home and Chip had done the dishes, I thought hard about Father's bicycle ride.

The next morning, just as he had all summer, just as we used to do together before my accident, Chip woke at five, put on his cycling shorts and shoes, hopped on his racing bike, and rode for an hour or two out the Haines Highway, which is really a gentle two-lane road along the Chilkat River. That afternoon I climbed on my town cruiser in my regular clothes: baggy old shorts and a T-shirt. (Although I stuck a neon cycling jacket in the basket, along with a water bottle.) I wasn't sure where I was heading. I didn't want to have a goal I couldn't meet. So I pedaled over Cemetery Hill, through the intersection where Kevin's truck had run me over, down by the boat harbor, along Front Street, and right out Lutak Road along the inlet. There were high clouds but no hint of rain. It was warm and calm: a nice afternoon for a long, slow ride. Before I knew it, I was at the ferry terminal, cruising by the rusty old sawmill where Chip once worked and winding down along the shady shore, up the cooler, gurgling riverside road, and finally arriving at Chilkoot Lake. I had seen only six cars and trucks the whole trip. I stepped off the bike and took a long look out across the lake. It's rimmed by spruce forests and high rocky mountains that keep some of their snow all year. It was empty and I was alone, except for an RV parked across the turn-around. A couple descended from it and wandered over, enthusing that it sure was magnificent, wasn't it? They asked if I was from around here. When I said I was, they wanted to know if I knew the woman who wrote the book about Haines called *If You Lived Here, I'd Know Your Name*. My hair is a lot longer than on the jacket photo, and grayer. They had heard she'd had a bad accident and wanted to know if she was okay. She was, I told them.

I didn't say that she was me. The last time I had planned a long bike ride I had been preoccupied with thoughts about the woman who wrote that book. That hadn't gone so well. I figured it was safer to leave her at home that day.

A few days later my dad arrived for his first visit since Mom's death. He looked thinner than he had at her funeral. I jogged with him on my now regular loop, but instead of running up Cemetery Hill, we slalomed down it, the way we had near his house, and as always, we talked. He admitted that staying alone in our guest room above the garage was the hardest part about being in Haines without my mother. He also wished he knew how to use the digital camera he'd bought her for Christmas a couple years back. He'd like to take some pictures of the farm and of her garden to show me; he's been keeping up with it. Then he asked if I thought my mother knew she was dying, and if I thought there was something more she would have said to us, if she could have. Like me, he had been wondering. She had hung on so hard to life. Maybe there was some unfinished business? "Do you think that she's at peace?" he asked. I said she was probably playing golf in heaven. "I wish I could believe that," he said. "I hope it's true." He hadn't been playing much himself; it wasn't the same game without her.

Then, on the Fourth of July, walking between the picnic in Tlingit Park and a mud volleyball game, Dad, Chip, and I ran into John Schnabel. John is older than Dad and older than Father Blaney, though just as active. He walks to the pool to swim laps most winter mornings. In the summer, he leads a crew with front-end loaders and dump trucks digging through the creek bed at his Big Nugget mine for the heavy gold pebbles and flakes that sink to the bottom. He stores them in baby food jars locked in a big black and gilt safe right out of a Wild West movie. I have a feeling that for John the value of the gold is in the looking for it, not the owning of it.

John was all alone out at the remote mine about five years ago, shoveling snow off the peaked cabin roof, when he slipped and caught his heels on the ridge cap. He lay there, on his back, feet up, head down, for quite a while and thought about his childhood, his parents, his brothers now gone, his children and grandchildren, and his wife, Erma. When you are facing your death and have a moment to reflect on it, this is where your thoughts turn: to the people who love you or who have loved you, the living and the dead. After concluding that his life had been blessed,

John unhooked his heels from the ridge cap and shot off the metal roof like a backward luge sledder. He managed to haul himself into his pickup and drive out the miles of rutted snow road to the highway and another twenty miles or so on to the clinic in town, where he leaned on the horn until someone came out and helped him inside. He had broken a few ribs and cracked his pelvis, but he made it to his eightieth birthday party on crutches and was back to work a few months later. He still shovels his roof. Before we parted, John raised his eyebrows and asked, "When are you gonna get back on that bike? Chip looks awfully lonely out there all by himself."

AT THE BLESSING OF the Fleet, my neighbor Betty Holgate looked awfully lonely, too. I watched her carry a palm frond up to the basket in front of Father Blaney as he called the name of her husband, Don, who had died this year. When we were clearing the land for our house, Don had pedaled over on his bicycle. He had replaced the stock seat with a bigger, more comfortable one, and since he always wore brown work pants and a matching shirt, he looked more like a farmer on a tractor than the fisherman he was. He could have been on the old *Bert and I* radio show, thanks to a dry wit and a Rhode Island accent.

That day, Don had advised us to build the foundation of the house the same as the hull of a boat, so it would float in the pea gravel when we had one of the many small earthquakes the Chilkat Valley is prone to. He warned us not to let the well driller go too deep either—that there was good water between thirty and fifty feet, but that if we were greedy and went deeper, the casing would go right through a layer of clay into the brackish water of the inlet and be undrinkable. He told us that the only trouble we would ever have with the well water was that the minerals in it sometimes clogged the pipes. Then he explained what to do when it mysteriously shuts off: shoot a .44 Magnum down the pipe to break up the mineral deposits.

When another one of our neighbors crashed his plane on the beach one winter afternoon, I called Don (he was a pilot as well) before running out with an armful of blankets for the survivors or, God forbid, victims. By the time I post-holed through the deep snow, Don had already helped the pilot and his wife and grandson out of the wreck—no one had even been bruised—and was organizing the volunteers from the fire department to lift up the plane's crushed nose and slide the whole rig up to safety. Before climbing back into his truck, Don observed that there are only two kinds of bush pilots: "Ones that have bent a prop, and ones who will." I think, now, that there are two kinds of people: ones who have had something bad happen to them, and ones who will.

Don was almost eighty when the wear and tear of an active life caught up with him, and he took a fall he never recovered from. He was not a hospice client—Betty prefers to keep "everything under control" herself, as she says, but my training and experience with Hospice of Haines helped me when I sat with them as he lay dying. I wouldn't have thought I could sleep in a wooden rocking chair, but I must have. I woke with a twitch and heard Don breathing, quietly and slowly. Then he stopped and I counted, "One one-thousand, two one-thousand, three one-thousand." I reached six one-thousand and was holding my own breath, when Don finally inhaled again. I was relieved. Letting someone go for good, even when there is no other option, is not as easy in practice as it is in theory. Don was under a pile of soft quilts made by Betty, who was stretched out beside him. They had shared that bed for fifty-nine years and she wasn't about to sleep alone until she had to.

It was strange, waiting for Don to leave us. It felt more and more as though we were opening a door and helping him through it, rather than closing one. As the hours turned into a day and the day into two, three, and four, he seemed to be moving closer to someplace we couldn't see or hear but could feel. The window above the bed was ajar. We hoped the sound of the stream flowing to the beach and the inlet flowing to the sea might help carry his soul there.

Betty and I talked quietly in what had become a holy kind of darkness, she in the bed against the wall, me in the rocker, and Don sleeping between us. His face already wore the waxy mask of death. We both wished that he could cross over into the country of the dead and then come back and tell us about it. Don was such a good storyteller. But he wasn't communicating with us anymore. We listened for his breathing but mostly heard Bart, the old Newfoundland, panting in the doorway. Don's kitten was on the bed, sitting up watching everything.

Betty didn't plan this home death. The volunteer ambulance crew arrived the night she needed some help. Don had fallen and couldn't stand up and she thought he might be down for good. After Don was stable and everything was less frightening, Fireman Al said Don might be too weak to survive a Coast Guard helicopter ride to the Juneau hospital. He also was pretty sure there wouldn't be much they could do for him there, either, and they'd probably send him on to Seattle. Al spoke to Betty and Don as the friends they were, and then he and his crew carefully carried Don back to bed.

Betty had called me after she dialed Al, so I was there and promised to stay the night. A saint of a nurse from the clinic arrived and performed the simple tasks needed to keep Don clean and comfortable. She left after assuring us we could call anytime.

Don's niece and her husband took the ferry from Juneau the next day, and more neighbors and nurses popped in and out. Sometimes everyone talked and laughed, sometimes we were still and quiet, and sometimes there were hugs and tears. Near the end, an old friend from back east called on the phone. He was not well either. Betty held the receiver up to Don's ear while his friend said he would be joining him shortly in heaven, but he needed a 1,200-foot grass runway to land his Super Cub airplane on. He asked Don to build it for him. I had gone home shortly after that, promising to relieve the night shift at 6 a.m. That's when Don lifted off gently into his final departure. Betty said he must have been waiting for something to do "on the other side." She also decided not to call the ambulance to transport him to the morgue until morning—there was no need to wake up Al and the volunteers. And for a few more hours Don was able to be in both of his homes, the one here and the one over there.

So at the Blessing of the Fleet, Don's name was called with all the other friends and neighbors who had died this year, and Betty walked to the front and dropped one of her palm fronds in the basket. She took the walk twice this year. Their youngest son had drowned fishing commercially for halibut when he was in college, back when she and Don were younger than Chip and I are now. Betty trod the path again, with the other palm, as Father called Jonathan Holgate with all those who were ever lost at sea.

I hadn't known that Don and Betty were married when she was seventeen and he was twenty until I wrote Don's obituary. "Everyone said it wouldn't last," Betty told me. After Don's burial a friend noted the closeness of their long partnership. They worked together in their boatyard and commercial fishing. Betty had a pilot's license, too, and they were both good skiers. "I can't think of anytime I ever saw Don without Betty. They were a good team," he said. "It will be hard for her now."

I'VE ALWAYS THOUGHT CHIP and I make a good team. I was almost resigned to letting him cycle solo. Then a few days after my cruise out to Chilkoot Lake, I woke early and borrowed Eliza's sleek Trek road bike, the same model as my old one, clipped her cycling shoes into the pedals (we wear the same size), buckled my own cracked helmet, and joined my husband on his ride. The sun hit the Cathedral Peaks, creeks dropped from the cliffs, and the pink fireweed painted the ditches. Everything was so right with the world that I wanted to sing, or at least say a little blessing, but I was gripping the handlebars too tightly and we were going too fast. I did think of a line from a Mary Oliver poem, the one taped to my bedroom mirror, about another sunny morning and the "lucky person who is in it." Chip had been right about my luck all along.

But there was still one more thing I had to do in order to close the book on all of this trouble. I had to forgive Kevin, the driver of that truck, for running me over. I thought I sort of had. I mean, I knew it was an accident. It's not as if he meant me harm. He just didn't see me. I also knew, since I said my prayers every night, that God would forgive my trespasses. Then I read an essay by

C. S. Lewis, who pointed out that when Jesus taught us to pray "Forgive us our trespasses as we forgive those who trespass against us," his meaning was very clear: God will forgive us to the same extent we forgive others. It takes two to tango.

THE PREVIOUS NOVEMBER, I had been answering questions from a crowd at a bookstore in Anchorage, where I'd been invited to give a reading, when a stranger asked if I had spoken with the guy who ran me over since that day and, if so, what had we said to each other? I told her I hadn't talked to Kevin but assured her it was just coincidence. I wasn't mad at him. "Haines can be bigger than you'd think," I said. "We sometimes don't see some people for weeks at a time."

I knew, but didn't say, that for Kevin the whole episode had been, in some ways, harder than it had been on me. He had told an *Anchorage Daily News* reporter that in Haines he would forever be the guy who ran Heather Lende over. I also didn't admit that since my recovery I had avoided the largest grocery store in town, which he manages, and stayed clear of other places where we might have met. It was easier for both of us not to be reminded of how closely our lives were linked.

After that book talk, an elderly friend who had been at the Anchorage store, a wise, kind, old-fashioned woman, sent me a note. In her familiar script, she wrote, "Although it is none of my business," she felt it was important for

Kevin and me to meet. She suggested that I "go into the store where Kevin is working, walk up to him without a word, and give him a big warm hug." She apparently realized this might be difficult, because "after that," she wrote, "you can just turn around and leave." She sent a note instead of calling on the phone so I couldn't argue, and so I could keep rereading it. She knows me pretty well.

Of course, she was right. I decided it would be the perfect way to honor the anniversary of the accident. It would be a great way to make April a good month instead of such a bad one. That would also give me plenty of time to prepare for it, since it was five months away.

We have Thanksgiving early at our house, because Chip and one or more of the kids—this particular year it was our youngest, Stoli—spend the week in camp deer hunting. I didn't realize until a few days before they were scheduled to leave that I needed to buy a turkey. I had ordered an organic one from Mountain Market, but since the real holiday was two weeks away, it wasn't in town yet. I called Simon, the butcher at Olerud's, the other smaller grocery store, but he said his turkeys weren't coming in until the following week's barge from Seattle. We could have moose or goat roasts. We could. I could make it an all-Alaskan-food kind of Thanksgiving.

Or I could bake lasagna. It would be a good story—I could say, "There were no turkeys in town and we've been eating a lot of game lately, so we're going to have something a little different." It would be funny, the stuff of family legend. Lasagna could become a Thanksgiving tradition. The only trouble was that there *were* turkeys in town. They always have frozen turkeys at Kevin's store, and my friends and family know that. We've all walked by them, piled up in the freezer like a boxcar load of boulders.

I silently cursed my do-gooder friend and her sweet-as-bread-and-butter note. It was almost as if she had planned this. Had she secretly hijacked all the turkeys bound for Haines so I'd have to go into the store where Kevin works? Did she know I wouldn't be able to forget about Thanksgiving? To just skip right over it to Christmas?

I had no choice, and this was becoming ridiculous. The more I thought about it not being a big deal, the bigger deal forgiving Kevin became. (There's a lesson there, too, but it will have to wait.) I was only a few feet inside the store when I bumped right into him. He was spinning around with a wad of loose cash register tape in his hand. I learned that it's true that God works in mysterious ways—either that or I'd temporarily lost my mind—because I was so startled I gave Kevin a hug. Then I even kissed him on the cheek and mumbled something about being okay and not to worry. This was so unlike me it was almost an out-of-body experience. Kevin's eyes filled and mine did, too, and I bolted toward the frozen turkeys. Or I tried to.

Kevin had not read my friend's little note. He did not

follow the script. He didn't know we weren't supposed to speak. He had his hand on my arm and wouldn't let go. "Does it hurt when the weather is cold?" he asked. "I mean can you feel it in your bones?" Sure it does, sometimes, but I didn't want him to feel guilty about that. "I'm okay," I assured him. I was on my way for a hike up to Lily Lake and pointed to my boots to prove it. Then I turned to go, but he wanted to know more and he was so sincere that I took a deep breath and told him the truth.

THIS IS WHY you should never ask me, "A penny for your thoughts?" You are likely to receive a whole bank vault full of them. Especially in April, especially when I'm watching and participating in a community memorial and open-air prayer service as thought-provoking as the Blessing of the Fleet. I stood there, as the last few snowflakes of the season floated down onto the wet pavement of the harbor parking lot, and made all these connections, sorting them out in my head and heart. I listened as Father Blaney called the final names and the church bell tolled. When at last it was all finished, I felt better than I had in a long time. I had survived another April. I was still here, and so were all these people. This time, when we all sang "Amazing Grace," I finally understood the words. I didn't focus on the "wretch like me" line, rather, on "Tis grace that brought me safe thus far, and grace will lead me home."

What I told Kevin in the grocery store that day, after

my heart had settled into a more or less regular rhythm, was that the biggest change since he had run over me was a good one. There is a deep reservoir of gratitude way inside me that wasn't there before. What I didn't say then, but will tell you now, is that it keeps overflowing when I least expect it to. It's why I didn't walk away from this year's Blessing of the Fleet as I had done the year before, and why, when the Presbyterian pastor caught up to me as I walked to the car and invited me to the church hall for "fellowship," I went and had cookies and smoked salmon and coffee with Betty and Father Blaney and everyone else.

CHAPTER **14**

Preying Together

Give us all a reverence for the earth as your own
creation, that we may use its resources rightly.
—Book of Common Prayer

If I had made that Thanksgiving lasagna, I would have used bear sausage. Bear meat is better than it sounds. The original *Joy of Cooking* has a recipe for it, on the same page with the diagrams of how to skin a squirrel, in case you've got some in the attic you'd like to get rid of and not let go to waste. The rule at our house is that if you kill it, then you have to eat it, so I'm not really kidding about those pests in the insulation becoming a savory stew.

My method for cooking black bear meat did not come from a cookbook, but from Chip's Tlingit brother John Katzeek, and I admit I doctored it up some. For a spring black bear tenderloin, I carved two thick round ropes of dark meat from either side of a large male black bear's

spine, trimmed off the fat, marinated it all day in a ce-
ramic bowl with soy sauce, lemon juice, olive oil, rose-
mary, pepper, and a handful of whole garlic cloves, and
then had Chip grill it on a low flame until it was just done
all the way through and the meat thermometer registered
the same internal temperature required for fresh pork.
You can contract trichinosis from undercooked bear meat.
One local hunter who snuck a little piece of pink bear
steak out of his pan, where it was frying up with onions
and butter, became as violently ill as a person can be and
still live to talk about it.

This may be the bears' revenge. Bears, some folks
around here believe, are the animals most like us. John
says that while we white people evolved from monkeys,
his forebears descended directly from bears. He also acknowledges no conflict in believing that and killing one
or two a year. Bear watchers—many of the best are also
bear hunters—will tell you that bears have personalities
like people. There are mean ones and nice ones, generous
ones and stingy ones, smart ones and not-so-smart ones.
Some local legends caution against eating too much bear
meat because it can make you crazy.

Eliza used to be a vegetarian. She eats meat now,
mostly game, although she once said she would never eat
bear, since she doesn't think they should be hunted. She
shared our fresh bear dinner, though, because her boyfriend wanted to try some. It tasted really good. And no,
it's nothing like chicken. It was tangy and tender, similar

to lean pork. We served it with local potatoes, arugula, lettuce, and spinach from the garden, homegrown rhubarb crisp, and plenty of Spruce Tip Ale from the Haines Brewery. (It's an old recipe—Captain Cook is said to have added the tender green spring growth on the tips of Sitka spruce boughs to his ales to prevent his sailors from contracting scurvy.) The modern amendment to Thoreau's famous quote may well be that wildness *and* eating food from sources very close to home are "the preservation of the world." In *Animal, Vegetable, Miracle,* Barbara Kingsolver's book about her family's year of eating locally, the general rule was not to consume any food that didn't originate within a hundred miles of their kitchen.

Usually when people speak of local produce or meat, they mean growing or raising it themselves or buying it from a neighbor farmer or small independent butcher. In Haines and Klukwan, agriculture is mostly limited to personal use. There are only a few people who grow enough extra produce to share or sell, and that depends on the weather. The growing season is short. If it is warm and sunny we have abundant harvests, but cool, rainy weather is not kind to vegetables. The good gardeners bring what lettuce, kale, or broccoli they have left over to the Farmer's Market on Saturdays, which is more of a crafts and bake sale. At our house we have better success as hunter-gatherers. We pick berries and make jam, catch fish, and garden, but raising animals and real crops is more of a challenge.

Haines and Klukwan are so far from the lower forty-eight that it's easier and more practical to hunt for meat than to ship up grain and hay to feed livestock, plus clear the land and build the barn and install electric fences to keep the wildlife out. You should see how quickly a moose can turn a ten-year-old apple orchard into a few stumpy sticks or the way even a very young black bear can rip the branches right off of a loaded cherry tree, not to mention how easily a brown bear can break down a chicken coop door. And, yes, you can buy beef and chicken at the store, but all of it is shipped up on barges from Seattle and grown or raised even farther away. Everything in our grocery stores travels at least one thousand miles so we can eat it. Cheerios have a huge carbon footprint in Haines. So it makes more sense environmentally, socially, and physically to find food closer to home. It also costs a lot less. That's why we eat mostly wild fish and game, keep hens for eggs, and grow a garden. Even my nonhunting friends enjoy moose, deer, and goat. But would most of them eat a bear steak? Nope. There is something about bears that makes them so appealing to watch. The way they move and play quickens your pulse and is slightly scary, but mostly in a good way. That, and a skinned bear paw is a gasp-inducing ringer for a white, waxy woman's hand.

So, now I'm going to tell you how it came to be that I was preparing black bear tenderloin. Chip and John were planning a black bear hunt, and when they asked me to come along, I did. I thought a lot about sharing this with you and it may be a mistake, as I don't want to become the poster mother for bear hunting and the NRA or the whipping post for PETA. I just wanted you to know what hunting baited black bears is really like. I don't think a lot of people hunt bears for dinner, so it's something you may otherwise never learn. Also, if you had been bear hunting all night, as I was, you would not be able to think about anything else for a while, either.

Scenes like this one stay with you. They play like a movie in your dreams.

John, Chip, and I leave in the late afternoon or, really, early evening of a long June night on which the sunlight would never completely dim. I am in the middle of the bench seat in the front of John's truck as we drive out the highway and turn onto back roads about twenty-five miles from town. We pull off the pavement and bounce along on rough and sometimes flooded logging roads, towing a trailer with a couple of four-wheelers on it. When the roadway ends, we drive the four-wheelers through alder and cottonwood trees, over dry streambeds and across gravel bars, gullies, and muddy, wild meadows. I sit on the back of Chip's; John has his own. (Bear-baiting stations have to be at least a mile from the road, but this one is much farther.) When we come to the end of the trail, we hide the machines in the bushes and tiptoe across the open river flats into the dark woods, quietly and carefully following an ancient bear path littered with scat and fresh paw prints, on top of bear-paw-shaped depressions in the muddy ground and even in the stone ledges, imprints that are so well defined they could be man-made stepping stones shaped as bear paws.

The first rule when you are in bear territory is don't surprise the bears. Make sure they know you are there. When I am hiking near bears I usually sing country songs very loudly. Sometimes I jingle small bells or clap my hands and shout, "Hey, bear!" But now I am sneaking through thick woods miles from anywhere, stepping over piles of wet bear poop that are growing increasingly frequent, and carrying ten pounds of aromatic, loose, slightly rancid bacon in a floppy cardboard box. Even though John keeps talking about how good that fresh bear will taste, I'm pretty sure this is suicidal, the behavior of insane people.

The three of us pick our way down the bear trail, through branchy gray alders, into the deeper woods, up to a bench where mature spruce and hemlock trees rise from a mossy forest floor that is mostly clear of undergrowth. There are still islands of snow in the hollows. The blueberry bushes, willows, and devil's club are barely budding. At the bait station, which is not a station at all but a hole in the ground by an old stump, Chip dumps the bag of dog food he's carrying; John pours a jug of fryer grease from the Bamboo Room over it, grabs my box of bacon, and heaves it into the middle of the pit before we make a run for the rickety homemade ladder tied loosely to a hemlock tree. We clamber up it about twenty-five feet to a narrow plank hammered between two branches. My heart is beating so fast and the men are so urgent about scurrying to safety that I don't have an opportunity to mention that I'm a little scared of heights and that I would have preferred a railing to hold on to. My foot is still numb from my accident and I don't want to fall and test the titanium pins in my lower back. Also, it doesn't seem as if there is enough room for the three of us. But there is no time for any of that. Before I can even think of all the reasons I shouldn't be doing this, we are sitting shoulder to shoulder on that board, way up above the bait, waiting for the bears to come. We are absolutely silent and still as cold toads. The plank is weathered and warped and not very steady. I calculate our collective weight—none of us is heavy, but Chip is six foot one, and I'm taller than John.

We left town at six thirty in the evening and it has taken us about two and a half hours to get here. There is no wind, which is good for us, since the bears won't catch our scent, but even better for the thousands of hungry mosquitoes. I'm spitting them off my lips when Chip silently hands me an elastic mosquito net head cover. He pulls one on, too. John doesn't. He scowls at us and then smiles, shaking his head. Apparently mosquitoes bite only white people. I'm sure there will be a story about this from him later, after we can speak again. Even though it is the first week in June, with the sun behind the mountains, it is cold. I'm wearing three layers plus a hunting jacket, gloves, a wool hat, and heavy socks and insulated hiking boots. I spritzed myself with bug dope before we left the truck. It is the organic citronella kind. DEET is not good for you. I'm thinking that maybe a death from DEET is preferable to falling from this tree into a pit of feeding bears while flailing at the bugs.

When I asked John on the drive out if he had partici- pated in the DNA testing to help trace the mummified re- mains of a five-hundred-year-old Native hunter—they've named him the Long Ago Man—who was found next to a receding glacier a few years back, he said he didn't have to; "We are all related." The Tlingit name of the Long Ago Man is *Kwaday Dan Sinchi*. His body was found by sheep hunters just across the Alaska-Canada border in the Tatshenshini-Alsek Park, which is between Haines and Whitehorse. He carried smoked salmon in his pouch. His robe fibers were dated between 1415 and 1445. No one is sure where he was coming from or going to. John thinks that is beside the point. "The best walks are the ones without destinations," he said. Remind me to tell John that he sounds like a Muslim mystic, especially the Sufi poet Rumi, who observed that the destination is the journey.

John's cousin wove him a spruce root hat that is an exact copy of the Long Ago Man's. John wears it at spe- cial events, along with the older regalia of the Eagle clan and the Tall Fin Killer Whale House in nearby Klukwan. John believes that bears need a predator, and he is it. He shoots only old males, or boars, because he says they kill the younger bears that should be breeding and because they eat too many moose calves. John likes moose for dinner, too. He argues that hunting bears is his role in the local food chain. "It's about the balance," John says. "Men are supposed to kill bears in this valley; we are the only animal that does."

As the three of us teeter on the plank above the hungry bears, John pulls a portable camp stove out of his pocket, assembles it, pumps in the fuel, and lights it on the corner of our platform. From his other pocket he takes out a coffee can a quarter full of liquid, removes the plastic lid, and sets it gingerly down on the stove over the flame. It will, he signs to us, attract the bears, and he raises an eyebrow and holds his nose, indicating that it will also cover up my bug spray perfume.

The scent reminds me of a birthday cake in the oven.

It also makes me sneeze. Or maybe the bear underneath the tree does, or the sow and two cubs to the side of us, or the long, rangy cub making his way silently toward the bait. Maybe I'm allergic to bears. We hold our breath and watch as one bear sniffs the greasy dog food, then takes a delicate lick. He pulls off a single piece of bacon with his paw, using it like a hand, and then tears it very carefully and slowly, nibbling one small morsel at a time. He reminds me of a raccoon. He must see us, or smell us, but he doesn't acknowledge that. Then I sneeze again. Not a full blown "aah-choo" but the smothered kind that blows out your eardrums. John and Chip stiffen and glare. "Sorry," I mouth. The bear charges the base of our tree.

At that moment I am very glad to be sitting next to two seasoned hunters with big guns, until neither one cocks a rifle. John gently shakes a branch and whispers, "Git," or something like that. When that doesn't work—the bear is now standing up, scraping our tree trunk with his claws and clacking his teeth—Chip picks up a marble-sized pebble from the small pyramid left on our bench for this purpose and drops it down on the bear's head.

The bear jumps back into the shadows. He is distracted, not by us, as we soon find out, but by the presence of two bigger bears. We can't see them yet, and won't for about a half hour. We can't hear them either, as they pad silently up the trail, heel to toe, on long leather-bottomed feet. The first bear is watchful and wary but continues to lick and nibble, slowly and deliberately, at the bacon and the kibbles. Another bear finally comes out of the darker woods, and there is a scuffle and a horrible sound, a garbled yell, a scream almost, combined with heavy panting and scraping. Suddenly the smaller bear is next to us, climbing up the nearest tree, only feet away. In a moment, we and the bear are looking at each other eye to eye.

This brings me to another question that I cannot ask Chip or John right now. If bears can climb trees, why are we sitting in one?

Still we continue sitting for a few hours, watching the bears come and go, eat some and chase each other, all the while keeping watch on our fellow tree climber, who seems to be taking a nap over there, when one big bear saunters in and scatters all the others. Chip and John make eye contact, wait, and look at it some more. John whispers, "What do you think?" and Chip stands and then kneels back down onto the board we are sitting on. John motions me to cover my ears. The explosion is the loudest I've ever heard, or seems so in that quiet woods. The bear yelps, takes a few steps, and drops dead in the duff with a thump and a steamy exhale. I hold my breath. My heart hammers.

We scramble down from the tree as quickly as we had climbed up it—there was still one bear above us in the other tree, a sow and cubs behind us, and at least one other bear just out of sight. The after-midnight sky isn't really dark, but it's dusky in the forest. Chip hands me his rifle and says, "Watch our backs," as he and John begin to drag the seven-foot, three-hundred-pound bear out of the woods.

Watch our backs?

I do what I'm told. Which means that there I am, squinting through a mosquito netting headdress, crouching and backing out of the bears' lair and swinging a .338 Winchester Magnum left and right the way I imagine a bank robber leaves a crime scene, except I don't know how to use the rifle. The blood flowing in my ears sounds like a river, and I'm thinking for about the fiftieth time this evening that this is a crazy way to procure something for dinner, that this is why God made supermarkets, when I see the shadow of the treed bear backing his way down. I tell Chip and John to hurry up. We are still whispering, though I am not sure why. The guys tug and lug the still-warm dead bear. It seems so human that I suddenly understand why John believes he is descended from bears. This one's head is tipped back, his big belly is up, his "arms" are over his head, and his legs are spread out. He is all floppy, too, making him even harder to move. If it weren't so deadly serious, this scene would be almost funny—we could be hit men for Tony Soprano.

When we are finally at the edge of the forest, they drag the bear onto a sandbar next to the river, and I stand guard again while Chip and John trot down to get the four-wheelers and the tarp. At last, they skid the bear carcass safely out into the wide-open river flats, far away from the woods and other bears. That's when John takes a sharp knife and cuts the thick brown fur and white line of skin, slowly and evenly from anus to throat, right up the middle. Chip slices the esophagus and the sinews that held the bear's insides to his back, ribs, and pelvis. Together, carefully and neatly, with bloody hands plunged deep in the steaming cavity, they scoop the life right out of that bear. The hot intestines flex on the cold sand. I watch them twitch, then look away.

It's a beautiful night. The mountains are silhouetted against the deep lavender sky and the river flashes like mercury.

"CHIP IS A PRETTY good cook," John said, over his decaf with Splenda a few months later at our kitchen table, "but he has to work on his bannock." That's a biscuit made of flour, salt, and water. I can't see how it can taste any better than what it is and assumed that it must improve around a campfire. John says Chip's needs more Crisco. John works on and off for the local tribe as a carpenter, repairing Native-owned homes and businesses, and he was on his way to fix a chimney at the end of Mud Bay Road.

"I'm going out where all the Mud Bay hippies are," he said. "Heaven help me."

I told him they weren't so bad. I live on Mud Bay Road and they are my friends. "Heck, John, *I'm* a Mud Bay hippie." (*Mud Bay hippie* is a term that originated on Mud Bay Road but is used to label anyone left of center.)

He roared, "Jesus woman, don't scare me." Then he continued, "It is not that they're hippies that bothers me so much; it's the way they tell people what to do. We welcomed them. The Tlingit people welcomed all of you, and all we ask is that you don't tell us what to do. They've got NO HUNTING and NO TRESPASSING signs everywhere out there—and out the highway now, too. That's no way to treat your hosts."

I didn't want to get in an argument, or even a discussion that may end in one. I have lived in Haines long enough to know that this is a tough one to win and more complex than you may think. So I let John go on. John has strong

264 I TAKE GOOD CARE OF THE GARDEN AND THE DOGS

opinions, and he takes a while to change them. He still thinks I am anti-hunting, even after I went bear hunting with him. And he is, as usual, mostly right. He says next time I'll have to shoot the gun. Though I have since learned how to use a rifle, just in case I'm ever handed one again and in a position to need it, I have never killed anything except a fish.

I also thought I'd successfully limited the dead-animal trophies to the kitchen, where goat horns and deer antlers line the walls above the windows. A print hangs, too. We made it with an artist friend visiting from San Francisco using a real king salmon. After we rinsed off the paint, we cleaned and grilled it. I call the decorating motif "Alaskan Fish & Game." But then mountain goat hides showed up on the backs of the living room couch and the dining room bench; they are thick, warm, and white. Now more antlers have been tacked up over the chicken coop and the greenhouse doors. But I definitely had drawn the line at stuffed heads, or so I thought. On their latest hunt, John helped Chip find a big Dall sheep with heavy curled antlers. They took it to the taxidermist in Whitehorse, and now its head hangs over our fireplace. My house is starting to look like Sagamore Hill, Teddy Roosevelt's home, which was full of stuffed game animals.

When Linnus the art teacher saw the sheep, she blurted out, "Oh, my God." It startled Tom's wife, Jane, who also exclaimed, "Oh, my God," but with an Australian accent. Tom himself countered, "What did that sheep ever do to

Chip?" You make concessions in a marriage. Everyone does. My husband stayed by my side for three weeks in a nursing home. He paid two thousand dollars in vet bills for a dog that his daughter loves but that drives him crazy. He goes to work every day and runs a lumberyard in this tiny town well enough to support us. The mortgage is paid off, and he gave me roses on Valentine's Day. He thinks I am pretty even when the March winds howl up the Chilkat River and I get that Walker Evans dust bowl look in my eyes. He still has that same smile he had in college when I fell in love with him. This is all a long way of saying that if he likes the sheep that much then I don't care if he hangs it in the living room.

When I told my friends that I preferred my spouse taking up hunting at midlife to having an affair, Linnus looked at the sheep more kindly, but Tom held his ground. "Tell him to get a girlfriend," he scowled. When Matt from the paper saw it he was pleased. "It finally looks like a real Alaskan house in here now."

I grew up on Long Island. Annual school field trips always included Sagamore Hill. I loved that house. It was enormous; the hall was big enough to hold a bison *and* an elephant. The idea that you have to kill an animal and stuff it to appreciate it is so Victorian. That said, I have named our sheep George Washington. He looks very much like the Gilbert Stuart portrait that used to hang in all public schools. The sheep's face is powdery white, his horns curl out just like Washington's wig, and his mouth is closed and set the way the first president's often was, in a little half smile. He seems to watch you, the way the best portraits do. "It *is* art," Linnus said after the initial shock wore off. "Especially the glass eyes." Then she stepped back for a better look. "It is a beautiful thing. Dead, but beautiful."

The steaks from that sheep were delicious. I wasn't there when it was killed, but Chip said I should come to the Brooks Range with him and John the next time they go. He said I would love seeing those arctic mountains so far from civilization. I'm sure I would, but the closest I've ever been to nature's heart was out on the river flats that night we went bear hunting, when I witnessed its guts pulsing in the sand while the quicksilver river kept on flowing and the sky turned every color of the sunset and the other bears watched us from the woods. In church every Sunday we ask God to give us a reverence for all creation, that we may use its resources rightly. I have eaten bear meat and will probably eat it again, but even if there were no grocery store in Haines, I don't think I'd be able to shoot one. John can, and Chip can, too, but I can't.

CHAPTER 15

The Music of What Happens

O come, let us sing
unto the Lord.
—The Venite, Psalm 95

I hope Mimi Gregg heard our women's a cappella singing group before she died. She was still in Haines when we sang at the Lighting of the Fort at Christmastime. The choir really needs an official name, and this has been an issue for us, especially since our counterpart, the Men of Note, has such a good one. Women of Virtue was a suggestion that was quickly voted down, as was Lyrical Ladies. So we remain "the new women's chorus, you know, the one Nancy Nash directs." We had practiced "Hark the Herald Angels Sing" and "O Come, All Ye Faithful" just for this event, in four-part harmony, but we're not a church choir. Instead of cottas and caps we wore coats and knit ski hats with headlamps on them.

We stood in the inky dark behind Tresham Gregg's art shop on the Parade Grounds waiting for the cannon to fire and the holiday lights trimming the classically gabled and porched homes to come on. Other folks milled around in the darkness. Milk jugs with candles inside them outlined the sledding hill where children coasted down and trudged back up. Then from somewhere in the darkness, up by the flagpole, we heard Jim Shook holler, "Cover your ears," and we all did, then waited. Nothing happened. (Yes, Shook really is his last name, and you'll see in a minute how perfect it is.)

"Cover your ears," Jim yelled again. One woman who was new in town wondered if that was really necessary since we were, after all, a couple hundred yards away. We assured her it was. Jim's three-thousand-pound cannon was originally designed to launch harpoons off whaling ships. It came off a sunken hulk in St. Michael, way out in western Alaska. The restored gun now fires on special occasions and is a fixture at Fort Seward. This neighborhood was once the first permanent Army base in Alaska. It was built between 1903 and 1905 and decommissioned after World War II, which is when Mimi and her husband and a handful of other investors bought it, sight unseen. Each firing of Jim's cannon takes a pound of black powder and a lot of old blue jeans. Jim packs the barrel with rags (denim works best), lights the fuse, and waits for the big bang. "One time I shot a pair of Levis clear over

Tresham's shop, probably the farthest any pair of jeans has ever traveled," he said.

After the third "Cover your ears," there was a huge "ka-boom," followed by stunned wows. I felt the shock wave on my face and the ground shift under my boots. The background was suddenly dazzlingly bright, as all the white and colored lights on the grand homes surrounding the snowy field were lit.

Tod Sebens launched some more fireworks and passed out sparklers, while Mary, Joseph, and the baby doll that was Jesus waited on the shop porch to perform a living nativity scene. I had not been aware of our choir's part in the pageant, of which our leader, Nancy Nash, seemed to be in charge. Turns out, Nancy wasn't, either. Holly Davis was supposed to do it, but she had come down with the flu. (Holly was born on Christmas and has stayed faithful ever since. Her husband is Matthew and their little boys are named Mark, Luke, and John.) Nancy is a born organizer so she jumped in, enlisting her husband, Dwight, to do the readings, and, instead of Holly leading the carol sing-along, our chorus became the main attraction.

The script was right out of Luke's Gospel—you know, the one that begins, "And it came to pass in those days, that there went out a decree from Caesar Augustus that all the world should be taxed." With each scene we sang a verse of the corresponding carol: "O Little Town of Bethlehem," "Silent Night," "Angels We Have Heard on

High"—and, of course, the two we had actually practiced and for which we had waterproof music (wet snow was falling in earnest). A couple of mothers herded dishtowel-hatted shepherds, tinsel-haloed angels, and gift-bearing kings to their places on cue.

I stood next to a friend who didn't know the words to all the carols. I was heartened to learn that I did. I owe this to my mother, who made sure her daughters learned to sing whether we wanted to or not. For all our young lives, we sang in church choirs and in school choirs and, this time of year, we often sang at New York area nursing homes. Now that I've been in one, I understand how much that must have meant to the residents. My mother, an alto, was in the church choir, too. I grew up assuming everyone sang and that singing was the most important part of church. For the twenty-five years I have lived in Haines, our church has been too small for a choir, so when Nancy began this community chorus a few months earlier, I signed up. As I stood in the snow, miles and years from where I first learned them, the words from "Greensleeves" and "It Came Upon a Midnight Clear" came right back. It's an odd feeling to be almost fifty and realize that something you learned as a child has paid off. It's almost as surprising as discovering a use for algebra.

Half the crowd missed all or part of the nativity play and carols. They were on the front side of the building, roasting hot dogs, or thinking about roasting hot dogs, on the bonfire of shipping pallets throwing flames that threatened to char a nearby totem pole. Ever since my accident I have made a habit of visualizing the worst-case scenario and how I will survive it or even help others to. On airplanes, I note where the exits are and actually read the card that explains how to inflate the emergency slide that becomes a life raft. I looked at the inferno reaching wildly into the sky. A volunteer fireman agreed that if the pole caught fire it would crash into the fifty-foot-tall lighted spruce tree, which would then burst into flames and fall down the slope onto the power lines, which, in turn, would send sparks over the derelict barracks building. The building is long vacant, so probably no one would be hurt, but the boom and flash of the crash and subsequent burn would make the cannon blast seem like a popgun. To paraphrase Tiny Tim, God blessed us every one and the fire stayed put.

My mother always made sure we read *A Christmas Carol* each December, too, and *A Child's Christmas in Wales*. She died concerned to the end that her Alaskan grandchildren may never know the words to English carols or the proper King James version of the Christmas story. Funny how this year we all heard both. True, they were accompanied by booms and blazes rather than delicately chiming handbells, but as St. Luke promised so long ago, there remains plenty of goodwill and great joy, and December's snow continues to fall on our little patch of earth with a kind of peace.

• • •

IN ORDER FOR MIMI Gregg's daughter Annette to have some peace over the holiday, it was agreed that Mimi, who was elderly and frail and forgetful and required round-the-clock care, would travel down to Ketchikan and stay in the Pioneer Home there, where her other daughter could check in on her daily. Mimi was in Ketchikan only four days when she died in her sleep. It wasn't really a shock, but it was a surprise. She wasn't ill; her family had not gathered at her side. She quietly exited life's stage without taking a curtain call.

Maybe it was the timing—over the holidays, which always remind me so much of my own mother—and maybe it was Haines's deep December darkness, which no amount of twinkling lights can banish (and, in spite of Annette's best efforts, the wind and snow had already shorted out sections of the Fort lights), but I had a heck of a time writing Mimi' s obituary. And it was a big one: Mimi was the First Lady of the Arts in Haines. Dying peacefully in the tenth decade of an extraordinary life is not tragic. What I'm missing most about Mimi is the way she was when I met her, and the way we both were when we were younger (she in her sixties; I in my twenties). I laugh now at how Mimi convinced me to direct the musical *Carousel* when I had three children under six and was pregnant. When I insisted I couldn't, she said, "Oh, piffle." I still know the words to "This Was a Real Nice Clambake" and often hum the song about geraniums in the window, hydrangeas on the lawn, and breakfast in the kitchen in "the timid pink of dawn."

Mimi's story is both whacky and typical of twentieth-century Alaskan pioneers. They were not what you'd expect. It is no doubt why Alaskans, especially women, remain so hard to pin to a type. Mimi could clean a salmon and cook it perfectly, and she was well-educated, cultivated, feisty, and full of wide-eyed optimism about the north country when she arrived in Haines on a steamship in 1947 with two small children (two more and a foster child would complete the family) and her mother, Regina Viccarino, an opera singer of French and Spanish descent. "Madam Vic," as she was called, was a genuine diva. Mimi was also named Regina and nicknamed after a character in Puccini's opera *La Bohème*. She held a Messiah sing-along in her living room some Christmas-times, something my mother would no doubt approve of. Her father was an ambassador in South America, and she grew up in New York City and Argentina.

Mimi (and the other "babes in arms," as Mimi would have called her pioneering sisters; for Mimi all the world really was her stage) came to Alaska to join her husband, Ted, who was part of a group of Washington, D.C.–area veterans who bought the grand old officers' homes of Fort Seward and the rest of the Army base. "The first summer was beautiful, fun, and exciting," her daughter Annette told me, "but when winter set in, it was wicked, wicked.

They learned a lot about credit, and how bad the economy was."

Later, Mimi would serve on all kinds of regional and statewide tourism boards, cheerleading for Haines and Alaska. But that first year Ted drove a truck and Mimi opened a gift shop, which she expanded into a travel agency. Over the years, she also taught school, worked for the legislature, and, as I do, wrote a column for one of the state's large papers, the *Juneau Empire*. Mimi was a shipping agent, too, and even the deputy magistrate. But all that was only how she paid the bills. Her passion was the performing arts.

She helped found the Lynn Canal Community Players and our arts council. She hosted a weekly show tunes program, *Matinee,* on the radio well into her eighties. She put on a lot of parades, concerts, and festivals and helped build the Chilkat Center for the Arts. She was the force behind the Alaska Community Theatre Festival held at the center every other year for about twenty years. Mimi traveled to Houston and convinced the American Association of Community Theatre Festival officers to choose tiny Haines for the national drama organization's biennial festival. She did it while they were stuck in a broken elevator with her. "In her day," Annette said, "guys would lay down in a puddle for her." When Mimi decided to stage *Damn Yankees* during Haines's sawmill years, she recruited mill hands and loggers, then taught them to sing and dance.

I can't even begin to tell you how gracious a hostess she was or all the gourmet meals we shared with an opera on the stereo and a whole crowd of guests in the living room — it was all seemingly effortless on her part. Maybe entertaining was connected to her love of performance. There's an art to creating memorable parties. Mimi even baked her own bread for its aromatic ambience as much as its taste — six loaves at a time, in the oven of the old woodburning cookstove in her kitchen.

My first summer in town, Mimi talked me into acting in a melodrama for tourists. We sang a duet together, about going way out west and finding "some place that's known to God alone / just someplace to call our own / we'll find perfect peace / where joys never cease." That fall she nominated me for the Lynn Canal Community Players board. I was thrilled. Turns out half of the board were newcomers. Our first meeting was at Mimi's house, and she was there, along with all the former board members. We all worked together. That's how she recruited new people to be involved in the arts. Mimi probably would roll her deep brown eyes if I told her that she was on the forefront of such popular ideas as "community sustainability" or "mentoring." "It's common sense," she might say. "Everyone knows that if you want something done, you ask a busy young person to do it." I hoped Mimi's window was open a crack that snowy night of her last Lighting of the Fort. I hope she heard us singing because, mainly, when I think of Mimi, from her operatic name to her radio show, I think of music.

A long time ago in old Ireland, the mythical warrior and hero Finn McCool asked his followers what the most beautiful music is. They answered with all kinds of sounds, from birds chirping and hounds baying to swords clashing and a pretty girl's laughter. Finn McCool waited until they had named all the finest music they could think of. Then he said that the most beautiful music in the world is "the music of what happens."

In my life, a lot happens while music is playing. I listened to those songs of Compline when I was in that Seattle nursing home recovering from my accident. Thanks to Mimi, I heard show tunes every Saturday morning when my children were growing up: she played them religiously on the radio. My mother may have been listening to opera when she was mostly gone from us: my father put a CD of her favorite arias on the stereo when we brought her briefly home, the day before she died. None of us could stand to have her at Mt. Sinai another minute, so we had an ambulance bring her home, up to the farm, and we settled her in the living room on a twin bed I had set up there. They say hearing is the last sense to leave the dying. My mother always had good ears. As an assistant principal of a Quaker high school, she was the one in charge of discipline, and students believed she could hear them clearly through walls. My sister, my father, and I sat by the bed, where Mom lay completely unconscious, and toasted her with glasses of wine. There was so little of her left to recognize, even the dogs were shy. Forsythia branches bloomed yellow in a vase, and sunlight streamed in through the windows.

My family was not as comfortable with home deaths as I was. My dad would not have been able to sleep with my mother dying right in the house. It was too hard. My sister agreed. So we called the local ambulance crew a few hours later and the volunteers, including a young woman Eliza's age, gently lifted my mother on the gurney and took her to the small hospital in nearby Sharon, Connecticut, where her doctor had a palliative care room waiting. We stayed with her there until after ten, and then went home to bed. She died the next day while we were out to lunch. As with Mimi, she exited privately.

At her funeral everyone sang, "O friends, in gladness let us sing / supernal anthems echoing / Alleluia! Alleluia!" It was beautiful, all those voices in the full church, but I had trouble raising the "glad strain" in my heart. I didn't sing with them.

I did sing at Mimi's memorial service, which was really her last show. It was at the Chilkat Center for the Arts, and Mimi herself was there, or at least her ashes were, in a pink porcelain urn that "wore" her pearls and occupied center stage. Her son Tresham said Mimi didn't believe in the afterlife. "She felt you better make the most of what you have, because this is it." He said that not having faith in a world beyond this one is what inspired Mimi to live so well. A former kindergarten teacher and opera singer who had moved to Juneau came back to sing a selection from *La Bohème,* and our women's choir sang two sacred songs, as well as the zippy "I Feel Pretty" and the jazzy "Someone to Watch Over Me." Nancy and Dwight performed a duet of "Goodbye Old Girl" from *Damn Yankees* that made everyone cry. Afterward, Nancy mused that a women's chorus was a fitting metaphor for Mimi's life. "She got everyone singing along, and in the end got us to do more than we could have done alone."

SUMMER ARRIVED THIS YEAR like a battle of the bands. At low tide, choirs of gulls and terns on the mud flats sang so loudly that I had to come in from the garden to hear what a caller was saying on the mobile phone. Last night the sea lions were rocking out on Pyramid Island; the low clouds threw their growls into my open bedroom window. I woke up in a kind of sleepy way and listened to my teenage and young adult children and their friends playing guitars and mandolins and singing out on the deck late into the evening. The cries of shorebirds blended with the strains of that same sweet question of what Aime wants to do: "I think I could stay with you / For a while, maybe longer if I do." Chip was sound asleep next to me and didn't move when I smoothed his bald head. He's tired. He's been hunting for hooters. Not the nightclub; rather, the birds, which are blue grouse. The males add to the seasonal din with a "hooo-hoooo." It's close to the sound made by blowing across the top of a deep bottle, only louder. Hooters can throw their hoots up to a mile, so you can't easily tell where they are by following their calls. The hardest part of hooter hunting is finding them, but once they see you, they don't move. They'll stay frozen even after you move in very close, which is why Don Nash said, "Even *you* could shoot a hooter, Heather." He was at the stove at the time turning strips of the beer-battered grouse in sizzling oil.

"No, I couldn't," I said.

"Sure you could," he said. "It might take you a few tries but you'd hit one."

That's not what I meant by couldn't. I meant I liked the hooter's song too much to silence it.

In the dusk of high summer, I listened for a "hooing" hooter and looked at the sign taped to my bedroom door. BRIDE'S DRESSING ROOM was written in light blue calligraphy. There was still a flowerpot in the driveway with a similar sign stuck in it announcing WEDDING THIS WAY and another one on the back door steering guests clear of the house because the bride and groom would like some privacy. My friend Frankie had made them. Her husband is the pastor of the Haines Cornerstone Foursquare Gospel Church, and Frankie decorates the library at Christmas. It's so pretty you'd have to see it to believe it. When she heard that our daughter Sarah was getting married,

Frankie asked if she could be our wedding planner. Frankie reads all the decorating and entertaining magazines. She said it was important to have a theme. I said it would be an Alaskan family beach wedding. She looked at my family, and the beach we live on, and said, "That'll work." Then she told me to weed-whack some of the sea grass down in front and to have the kids move those driftwood stumps to use as stands for the buckets of flowers.

While we worked, the sea lions exhaled with explosive wet breaths, eagles whistled, and trumpeter swans honked as they passed the house on their way up the river toward Chilkat Lake. The backbeat came from the putt-putt of a fishing boat's diesel engine out off Pyramid Island and Christian's dirt bike backfiring in our gravel driveway. I asked Frankie what we would do if it rained, and she said it wouldn't.

IF YOU'D LIKE, you may now hum "Here Comes the Bride," but we didn't hear that tune because Sarah didn't have that kind of wedding.

When the tide was just about high and the sun had burned off the morning mist, before the breeze picked up and while it was still warm enough to not need sweaters, just before I started down the beach rose-lined path from the house to the shore to take my seat on the picnic benches set out like pews, I thought I might faint. I am not a dizzy-spell kind of person. Maybe it was the champagne we had sipped a few minutes earlier while Sarah was dressing, or maybe it was the spontaneous tears between Sarah and Eliza that I had just walked in on, or maybe it was that I felt so fortunate, so rich in love—to borrow the title of Josephine Humphreys' book—that my heart felt as if it were a helium balloon in my chest. Maybe it was the spirit taking hold and making me fall on my knees in gratitude for being here, right now.

Then my son, Christian, offered me his arm in such a grown-up way, the same way he had at my mother's funeral when I had been suddenly unable to walk down that aisle to the family pew all the way up in the front. This time my nerves were happier. When we neared the familiar faces of our family and good friends, all standing out there in the sunshine, I said "Hi" and everyone laughed. I mean, it was still just my backyard and they were all staring at us. I know Frankie wanted a real procession, but this is us and we are not that formal. Chip and Sarah came next; all the while two friends played a classical round on the trumpet and French horn.

The horns were Chip's idea. He had been silent about the wedding plans until one evening a few weeks earlier when he announced that he had asked a music teacher and his gifted former student to play. After twenty-six years together he still surprises me. We had had horns at our wedding because my mother had insisted on "Handel's Trumpet Voluntary." That trio wore tuxedos. This duo wore clean jeans. But the music they made in that outdoor cathedral made me swoon. I did still manage to overhear Brian, Sarah's groom, whisper to his brother, "I'm so lucky."

Sarah has had a crush on Brian since they met on the softball field three years ago. Chip and I weren't so keen on him then, not because of anything he did or said, but because he is sixteen years older than she is. Brian, to his credit, sensed our discomfort and asked me to lunch so we could talk about his intentions. Brian is charming and I am easy to charm, so I sent Chip instead. "This is what fathers are for," I told him.

Afterward, when I asked Chip if he had given Brian the what-for, he said Brian bought him a beer for lunch and that, "He's actually a pretty nice guy." Then he put his arm on my shoulder. "Heath, I think he really loves Sarah and she loves him back." Just the way we did, and still do. It was like a country song. Only this was my daughter, and I was not so easily moved by reality. I was walking later with my friend Becky and doing the "When she's sixty he'll be seventy-six" math, when Becky said it would be a shame to pass up present joy for an unknown future. She said I could obsess about all the years between them if I wanted to, but I'd never know the sum of them. None of us will. Becky knows that's true, and so do I. He could die in a boating accident. She could fall off her bike. She could also live to ninety and die in her sleep. He would be 106 then.

Seriously, looking at Sarah in that white dress, next to Brian in his suit, standing on the beach with the sea and mountains behind them, and all the people who love them gathered close, I knew we were right to give her and Brian our blessing. Life is too short and too unpredictable to take a pass on love. Also, it is a great joy to see your child so happy.

Stoli and J.J. were happy, too, in the matching little blue dresses and ballet shoes they bought because they wanted to look like bridesmaids even though Sarah wasn't having any. They performed a song they had written for the occasion. Well, them and the Beatles. They used the tune from "Yellow Submarine" and added their own lyrics, such as "Brian loves Sarah more than ESPN" and "Sarah loves Brian more than the color blue."

Then Eliza and Brian's sister delivered the wedding rings, Brian's brother Brad pronounced them married (he's not a minister; this is Alaska, though, and by now you know this is how we do most weddings). However, Jan did give the blessing, including a traditional Irish prayer, and wore her collar to be sure it was official. After they kissed, we clapped, and Christian and Stoli played "Walk the Line" on guitar and mandolin. Someone opened a cooler full of beer and soda pop, and the cold cans were passed around. We all hugged and smiled while Nishan Weerasinghe from the lumberyard took pictures. Then the wedding party headed up for the bigger bash on the Parade Grounds, where everyone in town was invited to eat and dance.

The Nashes, with Christian deckhanding, had caught

some of the salmon, and Sarah and Brian's fisherman friend Stuart—who was once a star on my cross-country team—provided the rest. A couple of Chilkat River rafting guides grilled it, and all the guests brought a side dish to share. Frankie's kids ran around clearing plates and refilling platters. A bluegrass band from Juneau began at two and quit at seven, but the party kept going, and Brian and our kids and Chip's brother Steve and his wife, and our friend Liam, and well, just about anyone who wanted to kept playing and singing. Linnus was dancing with a dentist from Juneau who asked, "So where's your husband?" I wasn't sure what would happen, if Linnus was recovered enough from her own car wreck of a divorce to keep dancing. She shouted back, "I don't have one," and he declared, "Well, this is my lucky day." And they boogied on.

My dad told me my mother would have approved of the trumpet and French horn. This was just before he took his new lady friend for a twirl on the dance floor. They've been dating for a few months. As Dad explained when he broke the news, he's seventy-four and doesn't know how many years he has left, and he doesn't want to be sad all the time. Sure, he misses my mother, he said; they were married just shy of fifty years, "but life goes on."

THOSE AREN'T THE only changes. A couple from Colorado has built a vacation home next door to us. They brought in a backhoe operator to pull up the twenty-year-old trees blocking their view of the water and the mountains, then transplanted them between their yard and ours. "What do you think?" my new neighbor asked, pointing to the new woods.

"It's amazing," I yelled over the grind of the machinery. "Will they live?"

He nodded, yes, with all the authority of a brand-new Alaskan. "They do it all the time here, with ninety percent success." His optimism reminded me of Mimi, whose Christmas trees were always the nicest natural trees in town. When I asked where she found them, she explained they always cut two, drilled holes in the trunk of one and stuck branches from the other into them. That worked, so maybe this would, too.

When the backhoe was shut off and the crew had quit for the evening, my "old" neighbor, Linnus, whose family has been in Alaska for a hundred years, walked over to inspect the changes and share a beer on the beach with me. She is a grandmother now. Eliza will be her colleague at school next year. Yes, my oldest has been hired to teach first grade in Haines. I often wonder if my children would have come back after college if I hadn't been so badly hurt and if they hadn't had to learn so young that you can't count on the future. But just because you stay in one place doesn't mean time stops.

Linnus and I knew the meadow next to the salmon smokehouse we share would never be the same now that a home was going up in it, and we also knew it was bound to happen. But we didn't talk of that. There was nothing we could do about it anyway; neither of us could afford to buy the lot.

Instead, Linnus looked at the transplanted trees and my coil of garden hoses, took a sip of her beer, and said, "A mature Sitka spruce needs two hundred gallons of water a day." Then she asked, "How deep is your well?" Deep enough, thanks to another good neighbor we once had. A small plane took off way down at the airport, the tide flowed by Pyramid Island, somewhere on the side of Mt. Ripinsky a hooter hooed, and down the valley a distant avalanche rumbled. Through an open window, Stoli, who is Linnus's goddaughter, played "Stormy Weather" on the piano. Farther down the beach Christian and my nephew James threw a baseball, smacking it hard from mitt to mitt while a puppy raced back and forth between them, barking.

I thought about all of this, and a bunch of other scenes, too, as I lay there that night with Chip breathing beside me. I should take Frankie's wedding signs down, but I don't want to just yet. I want to be the mother of the bride just a little longer. I hummed "O friends, in gladness let us sing" and the alleluias that followed it, and this time I didn't cry.

The window was open again, as it usually is this time of year, and I heard the voices of our children and their friends who were singing down by the fire on the beach, as they often do this time of year. They were too far away for me to make out the words, but it's the music that counts, and I can hear it as clearly as the beating of my own heart. The old Irish hero was right. The most beautiful music in the world, or at least in my world, is the music of what happens.

Take Good Care of
the Garden and the Dogs

A Conversation with Heather Lende

Ten Things to Think about if You Are Hit by a Truck

A Conversation with Heather Lende

Heather Lende talks about raising a family in Alaska, being part of a tight-knit community, the role of faith in her life, and . . . chickens.

Your inspiration and your subjects are your family, friends, neighbors, and those who live around you in a tiny, geographically isolated Alaskan town. What's it like to write about people with whom you volunteer at the hospice, sit on local boards, meet in the grocery store, and pray at church?

Well . . . it's just my life. I've told stories from Haines on National Public Radio, in the *Christian Science Monitor,* and in a long-running Anchorage newspaper column. Because of our isolation, though, not a lot of my neighbors knew about my writing beyond Haines's own *Chilkat Valley News,* for which I write the obituaries. When I was working on my first book, one of my colleagues on the school board thought I was joking when I said I couldn't make a committee meeting because I was writing a book and had a deadline that day. Since that book was published, people are obviously much more aware of my writing. I hear "this is not for publication" a lot, and that's fine. At the same time, one elderly woman told me it was too bad her husband hadn't died sooner, because then he could have been in *If You Lived Here, I'd Know Your Name,* which was largely based on obits I wrote in the local paper. I'm also mindful of what I should say and not say. The line I usually draw, especially in this book, which was harder than the last one in that these stories are more intimate, is that if I'm at a public event—a funeral with 400 mourners in the local theater or the community Veteran's Day dinner where a letter from a soldier is read aloud—then I feel free to use that material. I am careful to present stories as my own interpretation of events: this is how it moved me and why. Also, since my time at the *Monitor,* I've always tried to hold to that paper's editorial guideline: "To injure no man but bless all mankind." But I wrestle with this every day.

Do you arrive at a community function eager for good material, with an active ear to the ground? And do you ever hope to head out of the house without tripping over a new subject?

I can't help myself. I always have a pen and paper in my pocket and often end up writing on napkins, basketball game programs, and even the church leaflet. Not all of that ends up being printed, though. Much of it is still in a pile on my desk. And, yes, sometimes I wish I lived in a place where I didn't know everyone, but so far, I haven't ever wished that there were less going on or that my life here were less . . . involved. One of the reasons my husband, Chip, and I chose to raise our family in Haines is for that very reason. We wanted to be truly connected to a community, with all the entanglements, responsibilities, and pleasures that entails.

What role does faith play in your everyday life? How religious are you?

I'm an Episcopalian, so that means I don't talk about this stuff much and I was a little worried about mixing it up in this book. But I wanted to write about my bicycle accident—I'm lucky to be alive—and then my mother died. I couldn't write about either of these occurrences without exploring what a large role my faith played in my responses to both. I don't think I'm particularly religious, but I am faithful and I believe in God. All my life I have attended church most Sundays. I say grace at dinner. And I pray, often.

Is life in Alaska your inspiration, or would you be a writer if you lived in, say, New Jersey? And do you see yourself as an Alaskan?

I would probably be a writer if I lived in New Jersey, but I would be writing about something else, and I suppose I would *be* someone else too. Moving to Alaska in my twenties, especially to this small town, has completely made me the adult—and thus the writer—that I am. I hunt and fish and snowshoe. My children were born here. The longer I'm here, the more grateful I am for this life in this remarkable place. I want to share it with the world. So, yes, I'm an Alaskan and an Alaskan writer.

Is there a "Heather Lende, the writer" persona that is separate from "Heather Lende, going about her daily life"?

Yes and no. My husband says no, but I know that my writer voice is my best and most polite self. In real life I swear more.

What do you hope to share with your readers through their experience of reading this book?

I've tried to give readers a window into a specific time and place and, by being so local and personal, tap into emotions they may have, too. This book began when I was quite literally run over by a truck, but if you think about it, by the time we reach a certain age, most of us have been hit by a proverbial truck in one way or another. Maybe it was cancer or some other brush with mortality. My story and those of my Alaskan friends and neighbors may help people see the value in their own stories. Also, I like to think I'm adding to the history of our time and place, like the pages put in the time capsule in *Our Town*.

In this day and age of homogenized housing, education, food, cars, and furniture, when so much of the country looks the same and feels the same, it's even more critical that we showcase what is unique in our own experience. Those of us who are able tell stories that aren't the same as everyone else's should do it.

One last question: I understand you have a chicken coop with the most intricate roof on earth. Care to elaborate?

My husband runs a lumberyard. I like to build things with his materials. I helped build the apartment above the lumber store where my daughter now lives, a cabin in the woods, and our house. I wanted the chicken coop to be pretty, so the roof is gabled just like our house, and it has shingles and two big windows so my hens (there are four at the moment) can see out from their roosting pole. The door was made with cedar tongue-and-groove boards, and I'm glad, because it survived two bear attacks, although now we have an electric fence that we turn on at night.

Ten* Things to Think about if You Are Hit by a Truck

The people of Haines were tremendously influential in my recovery, as were my family and my faith. Throughout the healing process, I was forced to look anew at so many aspects of my life. You don't need to wait for a near-fatal accident to take stock of what's most important, though. I've put together this list based on some of the questions I asked myself during this time. I hope these will help you start a discussion with your friends and family about your own spiritual and community life.

1. **Who will take care of your family while you recover?** Do you have friends and family who would step in during a crisis and vice versa? Have you talked about it with them?

2. **Who will take care of you?** What community are you a part of? Who are your main connections in life—neighbors, family, friends, church, political groups?

3. **Who is listening to your prayers?** Do you follow any particular faith or spiritual path? How do you practice it

so that you can draw on it when you get hit by the pro-verbial truck?

4. Why do we so often assume bad news only happens to other people? Is it denial? Chances are, in fact, that some-thing's going to go wrong sometime. Is it your nature to be an optimist? Can you ever be prepared?

5. Should you curse, or sing? How can your response to a bad bolt from the blue make you, and the people around you, happier?

6. Do you feel lucky to be alive? How does surviving trauma—emotional or physical—change you for the bet-ter? How does it connect you to your fellow humans, near and far?

7. Should you have walked instead of riding your bicycle? Would you get back on the bike after you healed? Why, or why not?

8. Speaking of healing, how do we heal? What roles do family, faith, gardens, and dogs play in our physical and emotional recovery?

9. Can you forgive the guy who ran you over? Why should you?

10. **What did you learn that will help you the next time you get hit by a truck?** Or when a parent is dying, a friend is ill, or a dog kills your chickens? What is the proper response to the sorrows in your world?

*And, finally (and this is just between you and me), did you shave your legs today?** Why do women care so much what other people think of them, even in an emergency?

Other Recommended Memoirs from Algonquin Paperbacks

If You Lived Here, I'd Know Your Name: News from Small-Town Alaska, by Heather Lende

An obituary writer and social columnist's offbeat chronicle of living in a tiny town ninety miles north of Juneau, Alaska, accessible mainly by water or air—and only when the weather is good.

"Lende offers touching stories about neighbors with whom she shares wedding celebrations, potluck dinners, tears for missing fisherman—all the joys and sorrows of family life in a remote town."
—*People* magazine

"Who knew a writer could find so much human drama, simple pleasure and thorny issues in such a remote place? If you like the stories on *Prairie Home Companion* or *Northern Exposure,* you'll love some real news from small-town Alaska." —*USA Today*

AN ALGONQUIN PAPERBACK TRAVEL/MEMOIR • ISBN 978-1-56512-524-7

Heart in the Right Place, by Carolyn Jourdan

When a fast-tracked Capitol Hill attorney volunteers to help her father, a rural doctor, in his clinic in the Tennessee mountains, she discovers that some of our greatest heroes may be those living right beside us.

"A beautiful memoir . . . Making a difference can be as simple as getting up in the morning and helping those around you."
—*Family Circle*

"An absolute delight of a book: warm, funny and written with great heart and understanding." —*BookPage*

AN ALGONQUIN READERS ROUND TABLE EDITION WITH READING GROUP GUIDE AND OTHER SPECIAL FEATURES • ISBN 978-1-56512-613-8

My Father's Paradise: A Son's Search for His Family's Past, by Ariel Sabar

Winner of the National Book Critics Circle Award for Autobiography, this sweeping saga of Middle-Eastern history is also an intimate story of tolerance and hope as it follows a son's epic journey back to his father's lost homeland.

"A powerful story of the meaning of family and tradition inside a little-known culture." —*San Francisco Chronicle*

AN ALGONQUIN READERS ROUND TABLE EDITION WITH READING GROUP GUIDE AND OTHER SPECIAL FEATURES • ISBN 978-1-56512-933-7

Join us at **AlgonquinBooksBlog.com** for the latest news on all of our stellar titles, including weekly giveaways, behind-the-scenes snapshots, book and author updates, original videos, media praise, detailed tour information, and other exclusive material.

You'll also find information about the **Algonquin Book Club**, a selection of the perfect books—from award winners to international bestsellers—to stimulate engaging and lively discussion. Helpful book group materials are available, including

Book excerpts
Downloadable discussion guides
Author interviews
Original author essays
Live author chats and live-streaming interviews
Book club tips and ideas
Wine and recipe pairings

twitter **Follow us on twitter.com/AlgonquinBooks**
facebook **Become a fan on facebook.com/AlgonquinBooks**